OPEN THE WAY TO KASHMIR

SOMDEV CHATTOPADHYAY

Dedicated to the Doctor of R.G. Kar Medical College and Hospital

Contents

Foreword

Young Netaji researcher and author Somdev Chattopadhyay's new book "Open the way to Kashmir" on Netaji's activities after so called air crash in the year 1945 is a very informative and pleasant book. A large number of documents and evidence on Netaji Subhash Chandra Bose are scattered all over the world till now.

Mr. Chattopadhyay's previous book "The Nilganj massacre" was also an important one to unearth the British brutality in Bengal just after the Second World War. I wish him success for all his honest efforts.

Jai Hind
Dr. Jayanta Choudhuri
05/01/2025

Preface

The first chapter of *'Wars and No Peace Over Kashmir'* by M. Maroof Raza reads: The Kashmir Valley is believed to have been a pre-historic lake. Indian mythology maintains that Lord Shiva and his wife Parvati helped in the creation of a dried-up lake and a basin-shaped Valley some 84 miles long and about 25 miles wide. In honour of the great sage Kashyap Muni, who had asked for Shiva's assistance, the Valley was called, Kashyapamar or Kashyapbhumi -and in due course came to be known by the name of Kashmir. Geologists have confirmed that indeed a great lake once existed, and a post-Ice Age earthquake shattered the mountains and dried the lake. There is also proof of Kasmir's ancient past in a Sanksrit document of AD 1148 by the poet historian Kalhana, titled *'Rajtarangini'*. It also tells that the victorious Pandavas of *Mahabharata* took to the Valley, and so did Emperor Ashoka the Great (274 to 237 BC).

Some historians think that India is the original homeland of the Aryans. They point out that in subsequent periods the Aryans migrated from India to other countries. The river hymns of the Rig Veda mention Ganga, and Yamuna at first and then mention the rivers of Punjab, the Indus, and the rivers of Afghanistan. The geographical order of the names of the rivers indicates their location from the East to the West. It has been pointed out that the river hymn signifies the migration of the Aryans from the Brahmarshi Desha or the Ganga-Yamuna Doab towards the northwest. In the course of such migration, they invoked the names of their gods, Indra, Mitra, and Varuna in the Boghaz-koi inscription.

"The Kashmiri language had no script of its own, rather it happened to be Sharada, a branch of Brahmin script used for Sanskrit from Kashmir to Kabul up to mid 14th century. Sharada was replaced by Devanagari for Sanskrit, but in Kashmiri Sanskrit itself got replaced by Persian as an official language in 15th century and

Muslim poets used the new script." -Javid, S. (1958). *Mystic Poetic Tradition of Kashmir: A Study. University Review.*

The promising land of Kashmir lost its independence when the Mughals annexed and joined it with their Empire of India in 1586 A.D; thus, from that time it served as the northmost point of an empire whose power pedestal was situated in Delhi. After their departure, it came under Afghans (1753–1819), Sikhs (1819–46), and then under Dogra's of Jammu (1846–1947).

In September 1946, it was reported that Russian troops had concentrated on the Kashmir border. At the same time, it was also reported that Netaji Subhas Chandra Bose was present in the North-West Frontier Province to meet the Faqir of Ipi, a tribal chieftain and the supreme authority in the Waziri uplands. Throughout the year, a number of news reports circulated that 'Bose is alive'.

Pandit Jawaharlal Nehru rushed to the North-West Frontier Province on his 'Mission of Love' for the Frontier tribes. He also sent V.K. Menon on a special and secret mission to meet one of Joseph Stalin's closest allies and Soviet Minister of Foreign Affairs, V.M. Molotov.

With Independence, the princely states, considering their geographical contiguity, had to sign the Instrument of Accession and join either the dominion of India or that of Pakistan. Surprisingly the former I.N.A. Commanders led a Frontier tribal attack on Kashmir. Pandit Nehru was clueless, fearing a third alternative was evolving. He said, "We do not know if there is any third alternative, because we do not know as yet as to who the invaders are."

The Dogra ruler of Jammu and Kashmir, Sir Maharaja Hari Singh sought immediate help and signed the Instrument of Accession to join India on October 26, 1947. On October 27, 1947, the Governor General of India, Lord Mountbatten ratified the Instrument of Accession and thus Jammu and Kashmir became an integral part of India. Indian Army was sent to protect Kashmir from the invaders.

The Army was quite confident of clearing Kashmir. But the orders were to "cease fire midnight 31st December/1st January 1948-49." Since then attempts by Pakistan to change the status quo have been repeatedly thwarted by India. Pakistan, however, continues to illegally occupy one part of Kashmir, PoK.

Almost forty years after that tribal attack, hand-drawn maps were recovered from Bhagwanji's belongings at Faizabad. Bhagwanj, also known as Gumnami Baba, was an ascetic who lived approximately the last thirty years of his life in various parts of Uttar Pradesh, India. Many people believe the ascetic is none other than Netaji Subhas Chandra Bose. The most thrilling journey of 'Open the Way to Kashmir' starts from the trails of Bhagwanji.

Acknowledgements

My doctor friend who (does not want to be named) insisted on writing a book on the subject about six years back, and of course, Shri Sourish Mitra who designed a thoughtful and excellent cover for this book.

CHAPTER ONE

Faizabad: The Trails of Bhagwanji

Bhagwanji hiding his identity, secretly lived in the guise of a monk at several places in Uttar Pradesh, including Neemsar (Naimisharanya), Basti, Ayodhya, and Faizabad. He kept changing his place of abode. He remained a complete recluse and interacted with only a handful of trusted who visited him regularly. He never publicly stepped out of his house, rather a room, and the majority of the people claim to have never seen him. He finally settled in an out-house of Ram Bhawan at Faizabad in 1983.

When Bhgwanji, who never allowed himself to be photographed, was reported dead in 1985, his belongings -largely books and correspondence in Bengali and English -were scoured through by the local police, and some kind of connection to Netaji was suspected.

In February 1986, Netaji's niece Lalita Bose was brought to Faizabad to identify the items found in Bhagwanji's room after his 'death'. At first sight, she was overawed and even identified some items to be of Netaji's family. A personal inquiry convinced Suresh Chandra Bose's daughter that the nameless saint was her uncle indeed. Finding that the state government intended to cover up the matter, Lalita moved the Allahabad High Court seeking an inquiry.

Bhagwanji's room was filled up with over 2,000 articles in 25 steel trunks. Lalita Bose, thereafter revealed in April 1986 to the media that her father used to confabulate with a rustic-looking visitor from Basti (where Bhagwanji or Gumnami Baba lived in the 1960s) to take messages from **"Subi"** -his brother. She rued she had not believed her elderly father then.

The court ordered the preservation of the belongings of Bhagwanji in 1986. Nearly two decades later, stating in its 2013 order that the "materials and belongings of Bhagwanji are national assets and must be protected for future generations", the Allahabad High Court directed that they be moved to a local museum. The court also suggested that an inquiry headed by a retired judge be carried out to ascertain the identity of Bhagwanji, "treated as Netaji by the substantial section of the public". In other words, the court saw credible evidence to kick start an inquiry to settle Bhagwanji's identity, because of his connection to Bose.

An inventory of his belongings was made following the interim order of Allahabad High Court, a copy of Suresh Chandra Bose's testimony and the original summons sent by the Khosla Commission to him were located among the belongings of Bhagwanji or Gumnami Baba. A copy of the record of oral evidence before the Khosla Commission by freedom fighter and Netaji's nephew Dwijendra Nath Bose was also found in the belongings.

Leela Roy, née Nag was a renowned freedom fighter, reformer, politician, and a close associate of Netaji Subhash Chandra Bose. When Bose was leading the relief action after the 1921 Bengal floods. Leela Nag, then a student of the Dhaka University, contacted him. She was instrumental in forming the Dhaka Women's Committee and, in that capacity, raised donations and relief goods to help Netaji. When Bose was Congress President, he nominated her to the National Planning Committee of the Congress. On Bose's resignation from the Congress, she along with her husband Anil Chandra Roy joined him in the Forward Bloc.

Leela Roy arrived in Naimisharanya (Neemsar), Uttar Pradesh on March 23, 1963, to meet Bhagwanji. She stayed in touch with him and kept providing for him till her death in 1970. Leela Roy's letters were also recovered from the items of Bhagwanji's belongings. She is the same prominent revolutionary Leela Roy who, according to a declassified document of the CIA, was a member of a secret *M-Organisation*.

Bijoy Nag, the nephew of Leela Roy nee Nag, appeared before the Justice Mukherjee Commission. He claimed that he met "Netaji" several times at Purani Basti and Ayodhha between 1970 and 1977. He said: "I used to stay there for at least a week during my visits. ...Netaji used to discuss national and international politics, art, and poetry during his interactions with me. ...There was an embargo on looking at him and only children were allowed to see him. ...He spoke about certain issues and events of Netaji's early life which couldn't have been known to anyone other than Netaji." Shri Nag also said that he lost contact with the person he believed was Netaji after September 1985.

Cloud over Netaji death papers

Statesman News Service

KOLKATA, April 3. — There is confusion over the death certificate of Netaji Subhas Chandra Bose issued by a Japanese doctor and it is too early to draw any conclusion over the matter. And the Centre is not co-operating with the Commission probing the disappearance of Netaji, too. These were stated by Mr Justice Mukherjee, chairman of the Justice Mukherjee Commission probing the alleged disappearance of Netaji in 1945.

"We are asking for documentary evidence of the death certificate issued by a Japanese doctor mentioning the name Chandra Bose. The doctor claimed that the certificate was issued for Netaji," he said, but added that "nothing can be said at this point of time". Mr Justice Mukherjee criticised the Central government for not co-operating with the commission. "The inaction of the Centre has made things difficult for the commission", he said.

The commission's recent status report was sent to the Centre for seeking reply in the form of an affidavit which should be forwarded by someone not below the rank of joint secretary. But, Mr Justice Mukherjee said, "They have sent responses signed by a duty officer. This is how the commission is being treated". The commission had also approached the British government which failed to provide documents related to Netaji's life. "They say they do not have any document. How is that possible," asked Mr Justice Mukherjee.

Mr Bijoy Nag, a witness appearing today before the commission, claimed that he met 'Netaji' several times at Purani Basti and Ayodhya between 1970 and 1977. "I used to stay there for at least a week during my visits. Netaji used to discuss both national and international politics, art and poetry during his interactions with me," said Mr Nag, who is partner of a publishing house which has published several books on Netaji. When asked by Mr Justice Mukherjee whether he saw 'Netaji', Mr Nag responded: "There was an embargo on looking at him and only children were allowed to see him". Asked what made him to believe that the person was Netaji Mr Nag said: "He spoke about certain issues and events of Netaji's early life which could not have been known to anyone other than Netaji" Mr Nag, however, said that he lost contact with the person he believed was Netaji after September 1985.

[The Statesman: 4 April 2003]

Shri Bijoy Nag's Jayasree Prakashan has published many books on Netaji. *Oi Mhamanab Ase* and *Oi Mahamanab Ase -Osesh* -these two books, also published by the Jayasree Prakashan are based on notes taken from Bhagwanji and compiled by Bhagwanji's most trusted associates under the pen name 'Charanik'.

Associates of Bhagwanji filed a PIL in Calcutta High Court to act on the disappearance mystery of Netaji Subhas Chandra Bose and following a court order, the Justice Manoj Kumar Mukherjee Commission of Inquiry was formed by the government in 1999. Justice Mukherjee, a former Supreme Court judge, rejected the air crash theory "based on robust circumstantial evidence" establishing conclusively that fake news of Bose's death was planted to ensure his passage towards Soviet Russia. Justice Mukherjee was not given access to some vital security and intelligence-related archives during his Russia visit and he couldn't tell what could have happened to Netaji after August 18, 1945. The Mukherjee Commission concluded that there was no clinching evidence that Bhawanji or Gumnami Baba was Netaji.

Journalist Ashok Tandon's inference that Gumnami Baba was Netaji Subhash Chandra Bose is also based on the fact that the handwriting appearing in some books and journals found in Ram Bhawan, Faizabad was sent for comparison with the admitted handwritings of Netaji Subhash Chandra Bose to Mr. B. Lal, Ex-Government Examiner of Questioned Documents, New Delhi has given a firm opinion that those handwritings (both English and Hindi) were of Netaji Subhash Chandra Bose.

It was Shri Amlan Kusum Ghosh who made a documentary film BLACK BOX OF HISTORY to uncover the death mystery of Netaji. Answering Shri Ghosh, Justice Manoj Mukherjee said off the record, "Don't quote me but I am 100% sure that he is Netaji." He was referring to Bhagwanji or Gumnami Baba. According to Shri Ghosh, that part of their conversations was inadvertently recorded. Later, Justice Mukherjee explained that the statement he made in thatvideo clip, was unofficial.

From whatever has come out in the public domain and what we have been able to understand from the statements of several people who were in touch with him, the man was preoccupied only with the thoughts of India's progress, her strategic interests, security considerations, and so on even as he engaged in spiritual quest. He chose to describe himself as Yoddha Sanyasi.

He sent a hand-drawn map and details of his Faizabad location in a secret letter to Sunil Krishna Gupta in 1984. Sunil Krishna Gupta is the younger uncle of revolutionary Dinesh Gupta who made a daring entry to the Writers Building to kill IG prison Mr. Simpson and fought a corridor battle against British forces in 1930.

Sunil Krishna Gupta was one of his most trusted and close followers of Bhagwanji, who had been well aware of his locations in Uttar Pradesh. Bhagwanji had instructed his followers from Bengal in 1983 not to make contact with him anymore. Following Bhagwanji's instructions, Sunil Krishna Gupta did not contact him in 1985. Then what was the necessity of Bhagwanji to write him a letter with details of his address in 1984? To convey any secret message?

Like other followers from Bengal, Sunil Krishna Gupta's belief was that Bhagwanji didn't die on September 16, 1985. If that is true, then whose body was cremated on September 18, 1985? There must be a cremation permit and a death certificate issued in his name!

Whether the local administration raise any objection to delaying cremation? How his last rites could be performed in a restricted area of Guptar Ghat? Why was Bhagwanji secretly or quietly cremated on the outskirts of an Army Cantonment that was not a cremation ground or shamshan ghat? Strangely, there is no death certificate, no photograph of the dead body, or the people present during cremation. There is no cremation certificate either. Bhagwanji's passing away was known to people much later after his supposed death.

The Bhagwanji believers had moved the court in 2010 and brought out a judgment in favour of their petition with the high court directing the Uttar Pradesh government to establish his identity. A one-member inquiry commission headed by Justice Vishnu Sahai was set up by the government on June 28, 2016. The report of the commission was tabled in the Uttar Pradesh Assembly in December 2020 and it said Bhagwanji or Gumnami Baba was not Subhas Chandra Bose in disguise but was a "follower of Netaji".

Handwriting expert Carl Bagget was given the two sets of letters to analyse without being told the identities of the writers. After he said they were written by the same person, it was revealed to him that the persons in question were Netaji Subhas Chandra Bose and Bhagwanji or Gumnami Baba.

Baggett stood by his conclusion and gave a signed statement to that effect. Baggett was an authority on document examination with over 40 years of experience and had completed over 5,000 cases.

Deposing before the Justice Mukherjee Commission, Sunil Krishna Gupta -who was an ardent devotee of Netaji Subhas Chandra Bose, said he first met Bhagwanji at Naimisharanya in Uttar Pradesh in 1963 and carried on meeting and correspondence with the seer till 1983. He said he had gone to Naimisharanya in search of the great patriot in 1963 after getting instructions from Suresh Chandra Bose.

The Justice Mukherjee Commission scrutinised the available evidence to a good degree. All this is in the public domain. More evidence has emerged in recent times.

When the Govt. of India took a policy to shift the regimental centers to the hinterland, the Dogra Regimental Centre was shifted from Meerut to Faizabad in 1976 and large-scale infrastructure was developed. Quite interestingly, Bhagwanji stayed in the vicinity of the Indian Army Cantonment in the same Faizabad.

The regiment traces its roots directly to the 17th Dogra Regiment of the British Indian Army. The British referred to all those who enlisted from Rajput hill states as Dogras and the first regiment of Dogras was added to the Bengal Army for the Bengal Province on April 20, 1887.

Battalions of the 17th Dogra Regiment (the 2nd and 3rd) fought in the Malayan Campaign of the Army of India. After the Fall of Singapore, a large number of the captured troops later went on to join the Indian National Army under Subhas Chandra Bose. Soldiers like Bhagat Ram of Himachal Pradesh, and Piara Singh of Punjab were in the Dogra Regiment of the British Indian Army who later joined the I.N.A. in Singapore in 1942 and died in action.

The Dogra Regiment is an infantry regiment and is one of the most prestigious and most decorated regiments of the Indian Army. They are called the Gentlemen Warriors. The Regiment prays to Goddess Durga at their regimental temple in North India. The regimental insignia is the tiger which is revered as the mount of Goddess Durga, who is a widely worshipped deity in the Dogra hills.

Netaji Subhas Chandra Bose was an ardent devotee of Ma Durga, Ma Chandi, and Ma Kali. So was Bhagwanji, who always believed in the highest force. He used to tell his followers about Maha Kali, Maha Lakshmi, and Maha Saraswati, their formation, and the supreme power. To him, Bengal and Mother Kali are synonymous.

Incidentally, the Jammu region, the abode of Mata Vaishno, is an area thriving under the shadow of the Trikuta Mountains which is mentioned in the oldest of Vedas -Rig Veda. It is one of the many in the region where the divine feminine is worshipped by the Dogras. According to the Hindu religion, in the Treta Yuga, when the earth was overburdened by the wicked and tyrannical rule of the demons, the Goddess Vaishnavi was created when Maha Kali, Maha Lakshmi, and Maha Saraswati decided to combine their energies to rid the earth of impending doom. Vaishno Mata is one of the most powerful Shakti Peethas or abode of supreme power in the Indian subcontinent.

The end of the Korean War was imminent when soldiers from the Dogra Regiment departed from Madras on August 19, 1953, becoming the first battalion of the Indian Army to participate in a United Nations Peacekeeping Mission abroad.

The *Malayan Tiger* was selected and a new badge of the Dogra Regiment was worn in 1955. It reminds us of the *Springing Tiger* of the Azad Hind Legion and the Indian National Army. Is it a mere coincidence that Bhagwanji most likely entered Uttar Pradesh more or less at the same time?

The Dogra Regiment played crucial roles in the Indo-Pak War of 1947-1948, the Sino-Indian War of 1962, the Indo-Pak War of 1965, the Indo-Pak War of 1971, and the Kargil War. This Regiment has not only contributed to the United Nations Peacekeeping Forces in Korea, the Gaza Strip, and the Congo but has also contributed to providing various military observers in various peacekeeping operations around the globe.

Bhagwanji claims that he had played crucial global roles in the Indo-Pak War, Korean War, Indo-Chinese War, Chinese Revolution, Vietnam War, and the Bangladesh Liberation War.

The Battle of Ichogil Bund was a skirmish fought from 22 September to 23 September in the Indo-Pak War of 1965 in which approximately two Pakistani companies attempted to re-occupy the eastern bund of the Ichogil Canal. The battle was notable for being fought after the cease-fire had been signed on September 22. The Ichogil Canal was constructed by the Pakistanis in the 1950s partly as a defensive obstacle to prevent an invasion of Lahore. It presents a serious obstacle for military forces.

When three divisions of the Indian Army were slicing across Pakistani defense and thundering across the Ichhogil canal to Lahore, British Prime Minister Harold Wilson sent a message to Prime Minister Lal Bahadur Shastri and Ayub Khan: "Both governments bear responsibility for the steady escalation which has subsequently occurred, and today's attack in the Lahore area presents us with a completely new situation."

Wilson's ceasefire proposal came at a time when India had the upper hand. In his book, '1965 War: The Inside Story', former Maharashtra chief secretary R.D. Pradhan narrates: "I insisted on military advantages being maintained. The UK proposals look like a trap." Pradhan writes: "In a way, India's leadership, out of its sense of restraint, fair play and endeavour to seek enduring peace and goodwill with the neighbour, seems to have missed opportunities to solve the problem." According to him, "The continued presence of Indian troops on the east side of the Ichhogil canal, facing Lahore city, was hurting Pakistan's pride." Moreover, Ayub Khan later said that Pakistan went to Tashkent as it did not want to risk a veto by Moscow.

At the end of a bruising 22-day war, India held 1920 square kilometers of Pakistani territory while Pakistan only held 550 square kilometers of Indian land. The Haji Pir pass was also captured by Indian soldiers after an epic battle. And yet India surrendered everything at the Tashkent Declaration in January 1966.

The army chief Jayanto Nath Chaudhuri was elevated following the resignation of another Sandhurst-educated general, Pran Nath Thapar, the army chief of the 1962 War. When the Pakistani cities of Sialkot and Lahore could have been easily taken after the bravery shown by Indian troops, Chaudhuri told Shastri: "We must move with the caution and wisdom of an elephant. We will take them in God's good time."

Here are *Charanik*'s notes taken from Bhagwanji [1]:"...*A wise man is one who can atone for himself by realising this fact. A fool is he who does not admit it. You cannot imagine the magnitude and intricacy of the events. Your brain will reel when you hear it. Where is East Bengal, where is West Pakistan, where is Tibet, where is China, where is N.W.F.P., where is Beluchistan, where is Indonesia, where is Africa -playing with so many events, can you imagine*!

You do not know whose shadow is over the whole of Asia -Mighty Cronos! Nemesis will come down. Mahakal says, *that now he has not to see what he didn't get, but what he couldn't give.*

And we innumerable countrymen are looking upwards like chataks (birds with a beak on its head that wait for rains to quench their thirst) *we have to see what we haven't got, we have to pluck from that nectar.*"

In *Charanik*'s notes again [2]: "*What you have written about* '**Inaccessible Places**', *in those directions where 'Mother' is called '**Ma-ri**': After hearing all these I 'raised brows' a little. What a great intellect you are! Carefully analyse those parts of the letter -the writings of this solitary pilgrim of the horizons, find synonyms, try to understand a few more times (Hopefully, then maybe all the things and topographies -logistics, the action of causing something -everywhere -you would grasp and understand, something -that I dared to risk, and intended to* *indicate the trails only to you)."*

"In return first meeting when Mahakal speaks, except in the minor stages, who can speak or ask a question? A strange combination of characters. Gentle in some situations, but relentless, and ruthless when working. This is a new man even though he is a man of the past. 'Acomplete break with the past,' while the man is unquestionably true. I will not forget the roar that I once heard -I have cheated death so often, I have been cheating death in every day of my survival. What have you done? 'Come Back' -is rhetorical. He will come back but he will have nothing to do with people."

"Visited for a day and a half...not 100% related to Mother Kali's Horizon, although with some scrutiny to know what to look for on the ground. So, it wasn't logical (and possible) to take Horizon along.

Charanik continues [3]: "Those commuting are poor, half-stupid, stubborn, and almost wild. My body felt old on the journey. ... Stayed merely for a day and a half. Despite the condition (illness), I had to go out again. Now just across the border. On the **Mari-Indus** *side, a special event took place. Knew him at 'one' time. He was fine then. The destiny of time brought him together with "someone very special". I knew about the 'organization' that I heard it do the work. Yet there was doubt as to whether they had attained such mastery. So, I had to go. They did their 'work'. On the first visit -more than one hundred and fifty shelters (Addas- or branches or 'what you understand') have been set up across a vastly extensive, hugely-densely-historically-encrusted forest-mountain-long (almost inaccessible for so-called white-collars). There are trainers in all those places (who come and go regularly) -trained cadres (they also go and come and go in rotation, and the people in between are being trained). For a variety of "work" environments and situations. A wide spread of that vast long area. Now and then the inhabitants of the hamlets are taught "how to do what and how to benefit themselves by it. Your system of governance is republican, in name only. More benefits as a result..."*

Decided to leave on the 15th, and return on the 20th night. When I went in the second time from there 'they' moved away and "did something" in a few other places in the same area. In that direction "they" will "move" for some time. Then they will move to other channels. For the "uncouth man to go to other channels (and help them) uncouthly, is impossible. Many organizations in those other channels are the fields of the Horizon. So, the "slightest inkling of eyes may convey a special meaning" -this eternal warning must be heeded in every step. So, moving towards it a strictly no. There "they" will stay for some time, it is not a good place, I went to **Mari Indus** (for the second time), but this time I did not go there ...a little below to the west beyond **Bannu** (covertly) there is a narrow mountain river in further west, along with the 'road' of the uncouth man to take shelter behind. He crossed the river. "The man" was (is) needed again. Travelled twice. Below the freezing point, gradually his legs became quite swollen."

Bhagwanji's comments on the Indo-Pak War [4]: "A dog who wins a fight becomes aware of his power to 'fight and win', and stands firm. (Started thinking. A strange thought of RELUCTENT-LINIENCY came) (It's only because of you Lee!) A few spinning clues, a few CUES given to a few... One went to a few places... lighning spread. (But, one was surprised and got frustrated... TO THE HILT, CUES WERE NOT USED).

BLAST IT ALL, LEE! LAHORE WAS COMPLETELY EVACUATED BY THE CIVILIANS, PAK MILITARY WERE FLEEING LAHORE LIKE SQUIRRELS. IT WAS A MATTER OF PUNCHING -A TAKING! ...*SIALKOT, MUZZAFFARBAD, AND THAT 1/3RD OF KASHMIR WERE A MATTER OF ONE WEEK.* "SOMEONE" WAS THERE HIMSELF. *SOMEONE* CROSSED AND RECROSSED ICHOGILL. THRICE HAD BEEN IN SHALIMAR! HELL OF HELLS, THAT THUMB-NAIL **AREA OF CHAMB** COULD BE LITERALLY-TURNED INTO A VERITABLE INFERNO, AND, NOT A SOUL TO CALL ALLAH! -DASH IT ALL! THEY BEHAVED (BOTH SIDE, INDIA Fankistan) JUST LIKE COPYBOOK PUPPET SOLDIERS!

Exercising Sandhurst SET PATTERN by both sides-MOVEMENTS -ETC. In other words, the authoritarians on this side could easily understand what they would do to each other. Yet, there would have *been 'something' * more (**seven more days, Kashmir would not have been a problem, Lahore would have been yours**) had it not been due to the bullying of "others" cum all of them LB, had not WILT! I could not imagine that Jayanto Babu would fall into the clutches of POLITICS.*

THE WORLD RESPECTS-VENERATE-FEARS ONLY THE STRONG. BE STRONG AND PREACH! : THE WORLD SHALL HEAR AND ACCEPT WITH ADMIRATION AND GROWING RESPECT. BE WEAK AND PREACH : THE WORLD SHALL KNOW YOU TO BE A REAL DESPICABLE-COWARD-HYPOCRITE FIT ONLY TO BE PATTED-AND BOOTED AND ENSLAVED D-MN IT ALL!

PAK ARMY COMMAND's main base just outside of Lahore was completely blown up... PAK ARMY could see they were losing everything (seeing the operations of IND-ARMY CUM AIR FORCE) ..."

[Indo-Pak War: The Battle of Ichogil Bund, Punjab Front, 1965]

Bhagwanji refers to an arrangement made to meet with concerned three parties, especially secretly, at a particular place and time but he suffered from injury or physical unwellness which he believed was caused by spiritual power to restrict him from moving and protecting him from possible life threats [5]: *"All the 'Sandesha' (news) reach you (Bhagwanji), he further informed that Sri Sitaramdas Babaji's (Sri Sri Sitaramdas Omkarnath was an Indian saint and a spiritual master from Bengal) health is bad and he would not stay. If you (Bhagwanji) had been in a position to move, you (Bhagwanji) would not have paid heed to any resistance and anyone's inhibitions. He would certainly attend the 'rɒn.deɪ.vu' (an arrangement to meet someone, especially secretly, at a particular place and time) fixed with those three parties. But after your (Bhagwanji's) return from that country, you (Bhagwanji) did not know what was happening in this area. This is the only reason; this is the only way to protect you (Bhagwanji). The blow was given in such a way and so hard that even if you (Bhagwanji) would have tried, you (Bhagwanji) couldn't have moved till the atmosphere of the crisis was over."*

Saying he couldn't remain present in the rendezvous, Bhagwanji probably indicated that he was not present at the Tashkent Meet!

*"In the RECENT fight, PAK got the motivation-encouragement, apt diplomatic support, and signals from the UK. When it came to **"grab the throat"**, DEAD GHOST thought the "INDIAN ARMY" was smeared with shame on the stigma of **"cowardly-spineless-running away heroes"** to the **PAK-CUM-UK CUM the world**. Ayub told LB in London **to his face**, "I CAN WALK OVER TO DELHI, ANY HOUR I WANT TO, YOU KNOW?"*

*LB did not (couldn't) answer Ayub in Pakistan many times showing 'great ignorance' (to us and the UK world) saying, '... Sha... What do Hindus in Dhoti know about fighting? They always know how to lose, flee, lick their feet, and enslave, this is a well-known fact of history. The SLAVES fought under the leadership of the British. **Will kick them and take Kashmir and Delhi at ease...** Will the guys be able to fight?"* [6]

Bhagwanji continues: *"Tashkent-proposals are prepared (without India's knowledge) before being made to INDIA. KNEEL DOWN of Pakistan after prayer-crying. UK (frightening PAK) runs to USA to "understand" the "right" thing, UK, USA, R. After the plan was prepared, he became the only friend of INDIA and came to the people (TO EXTRICATE PHANKISTAN AT THAT MOMENT AND TO HELP HER, BE STRONG FOR ANOTHER CLASH).*

Somehow this was communicated to LB and made it clear "PLEASE DO NOT FEEL SMUG. DO NOT TRUST 'R'. YOU ARE NO MATCH FOR THEM, THERE; INVITE THEM ON INDIAN SOIL IF 'R' IS REALLY" FRIEND AS YOU THINK.

BUT, HE LOST HIS HEAD. Pakistan GAINED WHAT IT WANTED. 'R' UK, USA... GAINED WHAT THEY WANTED."

Then Bhagwanji tells about conversations held between Lal Bahadur Shastri and M. Ayub Khan when they met for the first time -alone in a separate room [6]: *"Don't know if this news came here (I didn't read it in any newspaper) when L and AYUB met for the first time -alone, in a separate room, then AYUB said in Urdu to LB "Ab to Raham karo. Jo ho gaya so ho gaya."*

"Have mercy on me. PLEASE FORGIVE AND FORGET. Then proving India to be a strong elder brother and himself to be small and a younger brother, Ayub said many things to LB; Then he said, "... how can I explain to you that I'm somehow trapped, under compulsion..."

Was Bhagwanji suffering from Post-traumatic stress disorder (PTSD) and having upsetting dreams or nightmares about traumatic events? If yes, then how could he narrate every detail of whatever was happening around India, its neighbouring countries, and the topmost world powers unless otherwise he was thoroughly engaged with covert intelligence and military operations, and maneuvering international geopolitics for the best interest of his motherland?

It's quite unlikely that without being a part of a mission or a larger network, anybody could know what conversations were held between two high profiles in a separate room under the highest security protocols. If Bhagwanji is Subhas Chandra Bose and he couldn't remain present at the Tashkent meet, the 'Tashkent Man' might be the answer. Considering all notes of Bhagwanji true, it's only possible to gather delicate and minute details of the peace talks if any high-level agency was operating.

[L.B. Shastri, M. Ayub Khan, A. Kosygin at the Tashkent
Declaration, 1966]

In a photograph of Prime Minister Lal Bahadur Shastri,
Pakistan's President M. Ayub Khan, and Soviet Premier Aleksei
Kosygin at the Tashkent Declaration, 1966, a mysterious and
unidentified 'Tashkent Man', could be seen just behind M. Ayub
Khan.

An enterprising young London-based NRI, Sidhartha Satbhai
commissioned Neil Millar, a veteran of the Royal Signals Regiment
of the British Army, to conduct an imagery analysis on the still and
video imagery from the Tashkent Declaration of 10 January 1966. It
would appear from the footage that the 'Tashkent Man' had been in
a media role or a journalist, as he is frequently seen with a notepad.

Millar noted that 'Tashkent Man' is seen wearing a different attire, which might support the theory that he was present over several days. Millar focused his analysis on the facial features and ears that are available within the imagery and footage supplied. Millar's conclusions in his report by and large confirm that Netaji and the 'Tashkent Man' are the same person.

'The question arises that in 1966 Netaji would have been 69 years old but the 'Tashkent Man' looks much younger which is not possible without plastic surgery and or prosthetic makeup. If the 'Tashkent Man' is indeed Netaji, then what was he doing at the peace talks there, hanging around Prime Minister Shastri and President Ayub?'

Charanik writes [7]: "*...August 1965 to January 1966 is such a period. The various phases of the 22-day-long India-Pakistan conflict shook several crores of people in this vast country and many declared principles have been abandoned like worn-out clothes in the face of harsh realities. Even today, we have to listen to the false victory song of that failed policy.*

...After a lot of tension and many different comments, Shastri ji finally had to accept the Soviet invitation to meet Pak-President Ayub in Tashkent on January 7. In the face of the failure of the meeting, on the evening of January 11, shortly after the birth of the document known as the Tashkent Declaration, the Prime Minister of India, Lal Bahadur Shastri, died in the Soviet land in a very painful situation.

...Death! This sudden and dramatic death has shocked India and the world. As a result, the attitude and leisure to examine the benefits of the Tashkent Declaration was not yet been or wilfully allowed to happen. Some parties and individuals have termed it historical, although to us it did not seem to have any significance or novel value beyond the re-arrangement of accepted terms for UNO countries. Rather, in our judgment, India has been harmed and dishonoured if we exclude the idea of 'peace', the mantra of 'peace'. Pakistan is not only the aggressor in the Indo-Pak conflict, but

India's Kashmir region has long been an intruder in India's inaction. Yet the Western powers, especially Britain, nevertheless declared India as an aggressor with remarkable diplomatic firmness."

Bhagwanji says[8]:"...*THE NEXT "STAGE" SHALL CROP UP HEREAFTER. THIS IS TACTICAL. HORIZON IS (HAS -HAD BEEN) WORKING SO ACTIVELY THAT Pakistan SHALL BE FORCED TO MURDER KUTCH AND TASKHAND! YAHH HU RRRA HH!*"

"*YOUR DEAD GHOST HOPE THAT WHEN THIS DREAM OF GOVT IS BROKEN, (GOVT) WILL CALL "R" IN HIS VOICE, "SAVE THE GUARDIANS OF TASKHAND. FULFILL THE PROMISE. ...*"

Bhagwanji's remarks on Khan Abdul Gaffar Khan come [9]: *KH. A.G. KH. (Khan Abdul Gaffar Khan), erred in my judgment. What he is saying at this time (even if the common people are praising him to the sky) is not a sign of all that sharp mind.*

I was not present on "that day of yesteryear". But "that day" -"that situation" could not show the right principle and intellectual talent. The mistake he made at that time, is the result of it from then to the present. There is a great historical IF -his mistakes of that time. Of course, these are according to my knowledge. He is not only my adorable -but reverend also. ...

"*... Starting from Afghanistan and coming here many times in various ways -in his press statement from the reception committee. I will not accept the Nehru Award. ...I am not going to receive the Nehru Award. ...KH. A.G. KH is not coming to India to receive the Nehru Award. But...? (God bless him. Now he is 100% Indian leader.)...*"

Bhagwanji's trusted follower with the pen name *Charanik* writes[10]: *Charan feels, Mahakal was in India at that time (during the execution of the Tashkent Pact), and before that Deshnetri (Leela Roy) sent a Holland-made tape recorder (spool recorder) to him. There were many features in that recorder to meet the requirements of Bhagwanji. He strictly instructed, "What I want in the Tape recorder is that if it can be done in such a way that what is caught in its recording spool after pressing the key on it, will play the whole recorded spool and then it will play itself again until it is turned off. The power unit should be such that it can run for 6 hours a day."* Following his instructions, three electronic expert engineers, scientists, and technicians made it happen. Lee (Leela Roy) sent the concerned engineer to Bhangwanji to demonstrate before him.'

Charanik assumes, that the tape recorder was used at Tashkent, a recorded spool had been sent and it was possibly broadcast.

Is it a mere coincidence that the *Viswa Neta (Saptahik)*, a weekly newspaper reported sensational news on Bose's latest speech broadcast from Peking Radio at 6 PM on the night of 20-2-1966?

Charanik writes notes taken from Bhagwanji on August 8, 1967 [11]: *"It's been an amusing matter for the last 10/11 months. A GOC Punjabi was in the region during the last Indo-Pak war. A crucial rendezvous took place. The information that you have -he is not connected with.*

*That GOC asked an army officer (Akali Sikh) of INA to communicate with **SO & SO** at any cost. Pretending this was like a bolt from the blue -the INA Officer replied, but he is no more! GOC argued, that after the Indo-Pak war, there is no doubt that he is present. But the INA Officer repeated his words. Then the GOC said, I know it to be a fact that you know his whereabouts.*

The GOC was posted here by superseding two to three officials. There have been queues from him. GOC said, those who are in a higher position than me -are in contact with him (Bhagwanji). INA men wanted to know my (Bhagwanji's) opinion."

Barely A few days after Times Of India published a French intelligence report (of 1946) confirming the presence of Netaji Subhash Chandra Bose in Vietnam's capital city of Hanoi in October 1945, an affidavit was submitted by Arvind Sharma to the Justice Vishnu Sahai Commission of Inquiry, seeking a detailed probe on the above lines, especially concerning Bhawanji notes, which narrate the same details. Sharma in his affidavit dated December 26, demanded to specifically and strictly examine the issue as to whether Gumnami Baba and Netaji Subhash Chandra Bose were the same person or not.

"We also seek an investigation with regards to the credibility of the new evidence brought to light for the first time using the French intelligence report obtained by Adheer Som (logician and Bose researcher) from professor Christopher E Goscha", Sharma said. He added that Professor Goscha is considered to be an authority on Vietnam.

"The French intelligence file (10H600 EMIFT, 02B) in French states that Netaji Subhash Chandra Bose attended a six-nation conference in Hanoi in November 1945 and thereafter left via Yuan province of China for Russia and that the Russian government would have taken his charge from the frontier onwards. This proves that Netaji did not die in any plane crash at Taihoku on August 18, 1945," Sharma said.

A hand-written note of Bhagwanji obtained from Faizabad based-journalist Ashok Tandon (and listed as item number 1741 in the official inventory of Bhawanji's items in Faizabad treasury) asserts that he was "present in October 1945 in the South China region as General's guest and made contact with the Vietnam Government of Ho Chi Minh.

The documentary materials recovered from Ram Bhawan include copies of hand-drawn maps of Bhagwanji. Let us have a brief idea about North-West Frontier Province and its surroundings before we go into the details of one of the hand-drawn maps.

The Bannu Division borders the **Dera Ismail Khan** Division to the south and west, the **Kohat** Division to the north and east, and the province of Punjab, Pakistan to its east. Bannu District was one of five trans-Indus districts in the 'North-West Frontier Province' of British India. A description of the area is given by the Imperial Gazetteer of India: The District forms a basin drained by two rivers from the hills of Waziristan, the Kurram River and the **Tochi**, which unite at Lakki and flow into the Indus south of **Kalabagh**. It is shut in on every side by mountains: on the north by those in the Teri tahsil of **Kohat** District.

On the southeast and south, the Marwat and Bhittanni ranges divide it from Dera Ismail Khan. The highest point of the Maidani range at its center, near the hamlet and valley of Maidan, has an altitude of 4,256 feet. The Marwat range culminates in Sheikh Budin, the hill which rises abruptly from its south-west end to a height of 4,516 feet.

Political Agency in the North-West Frontier Province is bounded on the north and east by the Districts of **Kohat** and **Bannu**. North Waziristan District is the largest district in the Bannu Division.

Abdul Ghaffar Khan was the chief minister of Khyber-Pakhtunkhwa from the late 1920s to 1947. From the very beginning, he was vehemently opposed to India being partitioned and a separate Muslim state being created. He was held to be an anti-Muslim and even assaulted physically in 1946 in Peshawar as a result of which, he had to be hospitalised.

Realising that partition was inevitable, on June 21, 1947, a 'loya jirga' (grand assembly) was held in Bannu with Abdul Ghaffar Khan, members of the Provincial Assembly, the Khudayi Khidmatgars, the Pashtun tribal leader Mirzali Khān, and other tribal leaders in attendance. The 'Bannu Resolution' demanded that Pashtuns should be given the option to form an independent state, 'Pashtunistan', comprising all Pashtun territories in the region and not be forced to align with either India or Pakistan. After Pakistan gained independence in 1947, his government was dismissed by Mohammad Ali Jinnah.

Abdul Ghaffar Khan, a political leader of importance, became a very close friend and ally of Mahatma Gandhi, which earned him the sobriquet of 'Frontier Gandhi'.

In one hand-drawn map, the arrow points from **Tibbi** in Rajasthan's Bikaner to **Anupgarh** on the border to **Sakhi** and from there successively reaches **Mirgarh**, **Fort Abbas**, **Firoza**, and **Bahawalpur** in present-day Pakistan.

Keeping **Mithru** in Pakistan's Sindh province to the south-west, the Cease Fire Line (marked as **C.F. Line** on the map, and not the

India-Pakistan border line. This applies only when two countries agree to cease firing on the respective border.). On the other side, in the desert region of Rajasthan, **Tanat**, and **Kishnagarh** are bordered by the line, Ramgarh in the south-west, and **Birsilpur** (Barsalpur) in the north along the Cease Fire Line and **Bikampur** in the south.

The arrowed path from Mirgarh turns eastward between **Firoza** and **Allah Abad** and crosses the Cease Fire line into **Lunka** (Loonkha) village in Bikaner.

From **Lunka** (Loonkha), leaving **Pugal** in the south, the arrow turns northwest again and again crosses the Cease Fire Line to reach **Firoza**. From there **Allah Abad** passes through **Guddu Barrage** on the river **Indus** and crosses the river through **Ghazi Ghat** in the west (while **Dera Ghazi Khan** lies on the west side of the river Indus and **Ghazi Ghat** lies on the east side of the river) along the east bank to **Kot Adda**, thence through **Leiah** (Leyah) across **Sindh** (Sagar) **Doab** to **Mari Indus** and from there again to **Kalabagh** on the west bank to **KOHAT** by crossing **Indus**.

The arrow turns south of **Charsadda** to the west, turns south again, and goes round and round from **KOHAT** to **Dera Fateh Khan** and thence along the river **Tochi** leaving green mountains and picturesque village views behind.

After the confluence of the Sutlej River, the Chenab River flows to the southwest, crossing the marked **Panchanad** (Panjnad) **Barrage** (Panjnad is derived from Sanskrit words Pancha or "five" and Nadī or "river" which means "five rivers"), the **Chenab** joins the Indus and comes further to the south-west. In the drawn map, the Indus River is marked as **KOHAT** to the west and **ATTOK** to the east.

In the north, the **Sawat** (Swat) River joins the Kabul River near Charsadda. The arrow moves from **Dera Fateh Khan** to **Dera Ismail Khan** in Khyber Pakhtunkhwa, Pakistan, and continues to cross the border into Afghanistan and **Waziristan**.

Dera Ghazi Khan along with two other deras (settlements) Dera Ismail Khan, and Dera Fateh Khan are collectively known as Derajat.

North-West Frontier Province and Baluchistan have numerous passes at highly sensitive geo-strategic locations. These include the Sanghar Pass (Sindh, Pakistan) and the Indus River, and west of Dera Ghazi Khan, the Sakhi Sarwar Pass (Punjab, Pakistan) is considered an important pass.

Then, leaving the **Khost Mountains** (to the south and east of Khost lies Waziristan) and the **Safed Koh** Mountains on the left, the arrowed route crosses the **Kabul** River, touches **Sab Qadr** near Peshawar, turns completely in the opposite direction, and turns round again, crossing the Kabul River to the Kunar River on the Afghanistan border. The shore touches the **Chigga Sarai** of Peshawar. To the north of Jalalabad, the course of the **Kunar** River is marked, leaving the **Besud** (Behsud) to the west.

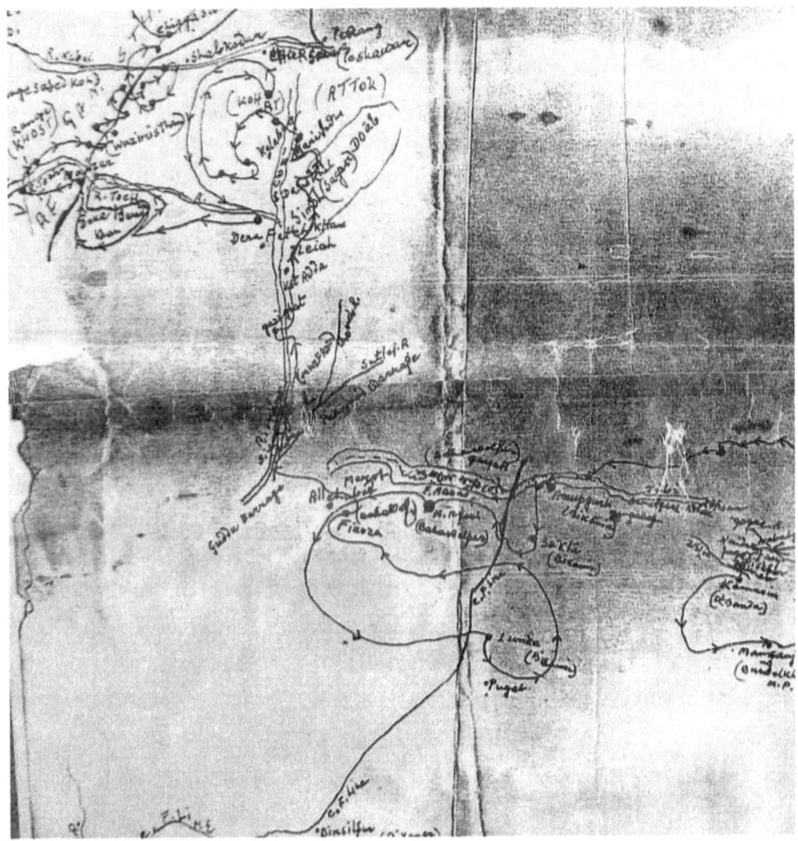

The marked path then proceeds northwards along the river **Kunar** and after some distance turns eastwards where the **Safed Koh** range is marked at 15,000'. Instead of heading southeast towards **Chitral**, the arrow leaves **Tirich** (Tirich Mir ridge) in the southeast and goes further north to enter the **Hindu Kush** range through the **Wakhan** corridor from Afghanistan to Tajikistan in the north. The height of the **Hindu Kush** range is marked up to 14,000' in the west, 24,000' in the north, and 28,000' in the east.

On the south of **Tirich** (Tirich Mir ridge) is **Dera Mandal**. **Chitral** (Chitral is a city situated on the Chitral River in the northern area of Khyber Pakhtunkhwa. It was previously the capital of Chitral princely state) is marked on the south of **Dera Mandal**. A line is also drawn along the River **Kunar** towards the northeast and marked as **(CHITRAL)**, probably denoting the Chitral princely state. **(GILGIT)** is marked on the northeast of **Chitral**.

Hunza, also known as Kanjut was a princely state in the Gilgit Baltistan region of Pakistan. Initially, it functioned as a principality and subsequently became a princely state under a subsidiary alliance with British India started in 1892 and continued until August 1947. In the map, Hunza is pointed as **(HANZA)**.

On the border between Afghanistan and Tajikistan, the Panj and Bakhsh rivers meet to form the distant Amu Darya (known since ancient times as the **Oxus** River, also marked by this name on the map). The route proceeds to **Rastak** near Jalalabad along the **Kakcha** river leaving **Mazar Sharif** (Mazar-e-Sharif) in the southwest. Further north is Fayzabad, the big city of Badakhshan.

Further north a place is identified as **Shiwa** (a large lake in Afghanistan has three names: *Kal-e-Shewah*, *Lake of Sheba*, and *Sheba*). From there **Kala Bar Panja**. **Kalai-Khumb** is a small place in Tajikistan on the border of Afghanistan. Formerly it was the capital of the independent Principality of Darvaz.

The southwestern area is marked as **(Badakhshan)**. It is one of the thirty-four provinces of present-day Afghanistan.

The path marked with arrows proceeds north, west, and northwest from the Pamir region to the east of **Kalaikham** (Kalai-Khumb). The **Panj** and **Pamir** rivers meet through the **Wakhan** corridor to form the ancient **Oxus** (Amu Darya) river.

The region served as a buffer during the British and Russian empires. Kala Panja village on the Panj River near the confluence of the Wakhan and Pamir rivers in northeastern Afghanistan. The arrow points towards 'R' (Russia) through the **Muztagh Ata** (Muztagata) mountain area.

Another arrow from **Mujtagh-Ata** goes a little northward along the course of the river **Oxhu** (Oxu) marked at an altitude of 25,000' from where it turns westward of the river and reaches the unnamed point. Another route marked by arrows comes from the east through an unnamed point reaches the **Karakul** lake on the China border in the northeast and returns to the unnamed point by an almost parallel route.

Stalinabad (Dushanbe) in Tajikistan and Uzbekistan to the north. Another line crosses 'R' (Russia) to **Alamata** (Almaty) and returns to a point in the south. The arrow marks **Badak** (Uzbekistan's Badak and Lake Badak to the east of Kyrgyzstan and Kazakhstan to the north and north-west) and the point crossing **Khari** from that point first northwards then much eastwards past **Alamata** (Almaty) and again enters **Karakul** on China border in Tajikistan.

The **Muztagh-Ata** mountain range is in the east of **Wakhan** in northeastern Afghanistan. Its southeast is marked as **Little Pamir**. This **Little Pamir** is a grassy valley shaped like a 'U'. The Soviets occupied the eastern side of Wakhan on this route.

It's difficult to know about the covert operations of the saint warrior, Netaji Subhas Chandra Bose in North West Frontier Province, Afghanistan, Russian territory, the North West, and the Nothern part of British India.

Neither the hope of Pakhtuns to be a part of undivided India nor their later desperation for forming independent Pakhtunistan was fulfilled. Quite unfortunately India was divided into two dominions -India and Pakistan.

Several news were reported about Bose being alive -in Russia, in Frontier, or other places. Soon there was a tribal uprising from the North-West Frontier Province. Certain reports confirmed that ex-I.N.A. commanders who moved to Pakistan after the partition were leading the tribes in certain areas. Afghanistan decided not to intervene and soon Maharaja Hari Singh of Kashmir decided to accede to India.

The Indo-Pakistan War of 1965 was an armed conflict between Pakistan and India that took place from August to September of that year. The conflict began following Pakistan's Operation Gibraltar, which was designed to infiltrate forces into Jammu and Kashmir to precipitate an insurgency against India. When India was regaining its grounds, a sudden ceasefire was declared and the Tashkent Pact was signed between the two countries. As a result, a vast area of Jammu and Kashmir remains occupied and controlled by Pakistan.

The trails of Bhagwanji recovered from Ram Bhawan, Faizabad give a clear hint that the old Fakir knew every detail of a vast geographical area, and sensitive geo-strategic locations, was well versed with war strategies to be taken in certain geo-political situations, international relations, and knew world political figures. Who could be he, other than Netaji Subhas Chandra Bose himself?

CHAPTER TWO

The Secret of "M-Organization"

When the German armies started their military drive eastward, German ambitions to link the German and Japanese forces seemed within the realm of possibility. In anticipation, the German Intelligence Service (GIS) made India one of its targets. GIS activities against India were directed from operational bases in Kabul and Bangkok. Its principal aims were the neutralisation of British rule by tribal uprisings, sabotage; and other subversive activities against British and Indian troops, to prevent their participation in the North African and Far Eastern campaigns, another aim was the preparation for a general uprising in India to coincide with the arrival of German and Japanese military forces.

To achieve these objectives, the GIS enlisted the cooperation of Subhas Chandra Bose and other exiled Indian nationalist leaders and their groups such as (a) the "All India Forward Bloc founded by Bose; (b) the "M-Organization", a subversive organization composed of "All India Forward Bloc members as well as members of other left-wing and radical groups; (c) independent tribes in the Indian North-West in Baluchistan, and (d) Indian nationalist leaders in the Far East leading radical groups; and their supporters in the Far East.

With Bose's help, the GIS achieved considerable success in India with a minimum of material and financial expenditure. However, Germany failed to take full advantage of the opportunities offered, and the GIS was particularly handicapped by the failure of the German Government to guarantee India its independence. Presumably, partly because of the lack of assurance, Bose left Germany and went to Japan in May 1943.

Besides Bose, Ali Mullah, Habibur Rahman, A.C.N. Nambiar, and Sardar Sant Singh were prominent Indian leaders in Germany during the war. Mohammed Iqbal Shedai considered the second most influential Indian leader in European exile, was chief of the office concerned with Indian matters at the Indian Foreign Ministry in Rome and also actively cooperated with the GIS.

In June 1941 Capt. Dietrich Witzel arrived in Kabul. Indian operations from Commercial Attache 'RASMUSS' had been working to build up an agent network in India. 'RASMUSS' remained in Kabul to assist and advise Witzel. After reliable contact was established with the "M-Organizaton", a steady flow of information came into the GIS base at Kabul about "M-Organzaion" activities, military situation reports, international Indian political news, and assorted other topics ranging geographically as far as New Zealand and Australia. This contact and communication channel had originally been set up in February 1941 when Bose had passed through Kabul while waiting for his Soviet transit visa. About 200 other Indian leaders had sought refuge in the North-West Frontier Provinces (NWFP) and Afghanistan. Among them were two prominent "M-Organization" leaders, Rahmat Khan and Sodhi, with whom 'RASMUSS' had been able to establish contact. Rahmat Khan became the GIS's principal agent for operations out of Afghanistan and its main link with the "M-Organization".

The "Forward Bloc" in India was directed by a Central Committee to which Subhas Chandra Bose issued directions through the GIS and Rahmat Khan. On this Central Committee were Sarat Bakshi, Abdur

Rahman, Narayan Chakravarty, Kushal Khan, Leela Roy, Bapat, Kamath, and Gujaram Singh.

In March 1942, Sodhi, a member of the "M-Organization" was arrested and revealed to British Indian security authorities the existence of the organization. In July and August 1942, the British arrested all leading Congress Party members and all known "Forward Bloc and "M-Organization" leaders including Lala Shankarlal, Shanti Ganguly, Sardarji Triptia, Ramkishen Khatri, Haidar Yacub, Abdur Rahman, Ashrafudin Choudhury, Kamath, Leela Roy, Narayan Chakravarty, Gujaram Singh, Mausamdar Datta, Jaiprakash Narayan. According to the CIA, Leela Roy, an acquaintance of Subhas Chandra Bose and a member of the "Central Committee" in 1942 was presumably a member of the "M-Organisation". She was arrested in January 1943. CIA presumed that Anil Roy was also a member of the "M-Organisation".

Several "M-Orgasnisation" members were allegedly tortured into revealing information that compromised the organization. The "Forward Bloc" was officially banned and forced to go underground but a new central committee was organized composed of the following five members: Rahmat Khan, Ram Sing Dutt, Ram Manohar Lohia, Mausamdar Datta, and Jai Prakash Narayan, the latter two having escaped from prison. About that time the "M-Organization" made political arrangements whereby it managed to gain the cooperation of the secret "Congress Committee", which led the All India Congress Party. Thus, the newly organized "M-Organaization" consolidated the GIS' earlier infiltrations of the "Forward Bloc"; the Kirti Kisan, a radical farmers organisation; the Congress Socialist Party; the Bengal Volunteers and the "Red Shirts" political groups. This enlarged organisation was led by the "Indian National Revolutionary Committee" (INRC) in which all factions and groups were represented. The INRC was located in New Delhi but also maintained a committee on provincial and town levels.

Ram Manohar Lohya was Secretary General of the INRC and the following, "Forward Blce" participants had similar positions on a provincial committee level: Mausamdar Datta, Jay Prakash Narayan, Gujaram Singh, Swami Sahajananda, Bapat, Ranga.

Sabotage schools were organized in which Joseph Shukla and Sachindra Sanyal were the chief instructors in New Delhi. Subversive work within the Indian Army was intensified by the INRC sabotage and guerrilla "Fighting Section" under Santa Singh. The "Administration Section" of the INRC was headed by one individual Yajnik.

Anticipating the possibility that its Kabul operations might be forced underground, the GIS, through Captain Witzel recruited two men as alternate communications channels between the "M-Organization" and GIS Headquarters in Berlin. They were Purushottam Das and Mukund Lal, two brothers whose business provided genuine cover for frequent travel between Teheran and Peshawar. The brothers also served successfully in the communications channel.

In 1942 Wendler was sent to Bangkok to take over Enovoy Thomas's duties and was joined by German Col. Scholl, presumably of the Abwehr, and SD officer Huber. At about that time, the GIS and the GFM recognized the need for better coordination of the various Indian nationalist groups in the Far East and agreed to the transfer of Subhas Chandra Bose to Tokyo to take over the direction of these groups. Before Bose arrived, however, the Japanese continued their efforts to gain control of the various groups and invited many leaders, including officers of the "Free Indian Army" to Japan for political conferences. The talks resulted in the selection of Subhas Chandra Bose as leader and Rashehari Bose as deputy for the group.

Two months after that conference, the Japanese Intelligence Service succeeded in merging the "Indian Independence League" and the "Indian National Committee". Leader Debnath Das was in active contact with GIS operative Meyer. The following month a Pan-India Conference, attended by Indian delegates from the entire Southeast Asian and Pacific area, was held in Bangkok under the chairmanship of Raghavan, of Malaya. This resulted in the founding of another organisation, the new "Indian Independence League". Raghavan, Penang, Menon, Capt. Mohon Singh and Capt. Gilani was elected as the "Court of Action" to direct the League. Subordinate to the "Court of Action" was the "Indian National Army" with Capt. Mohon Singh commanding officer. Japanese Col. Iwaguro informed Col. Scholl of the outcome of the conference and used the occasion to review Japanese desires for greater cooperation and exchange of information with the various GIS bases throughout the area.

GIS contact with Baluchistan tribal leader Hassan Khan was established in February 1942, using Subhan Khan as cut out. That year Subhan Khan was arrested by the Afghan police which not only endangered contact with Subhan Khan but also his residence in Kabul which was used by Rahamat Khan. CIA says that the Hur Moslem Brotherhood also co-operated closely with the "M-Organisation".

In July 1942, Menado in Singapore took over leadership of the newly formed "Indian Independence League" and the GIS contact Debnath Das became its Secretary General. Meanwhile, the Japanese IntelligenceService continued to build up the "Indian National Army", Mohan Singh, its commanding officer, was arrested and replaced by Kiahni. The Chief of Staff, Col. Gilani was arrested on suspicion of being a British agent and his associates fled to India Despite these difficulties, the "Indian National Army" reached an active strength of about 16,000 men, including about 500 intelligence agents, 200 of whom achieved limited success on missions inside India.

Close co-ordination and co-operation, however, between the GIS and the Japanese Intelligence Service on Indian operations did not become a reality until May 1943 when Subhas Chandra Bose finally arrived in Tokyo. German Navy Capt. Von Rueckteschell, assigned to the GIS, was stationed in Singapore and acted as liaison with the Bose apparatus. In addition, while in Tokyo, Bose also sent instructions to Rahmad Khan and A.C.N. Nambiar, using German Ambassador Stahmer and his GFM facilities as an alternate channel of communication.

Apart from Indian operations, SD officer Col. Josef Meisinger worked in Shanghai and presumably also in Japan. His specific activities could not be determined by the CIA at that time, although there is one document showing that he declined to recruit the notorious international intelligence agent Trebitsch Lincoln, who reportedly volunteered his services to the GIS in May 1941.

Most of the tribes inhabiting the northern regions of India and the Indo-Afghan areas had intermittently fought British Indian forces for years and were, thus allies of the Axis powers when World War II began.

Sometime before 1941, Anzilotti, chief of Italian intelligence operations in Kabul under diplomatic cover as -Counselor of Legation there, contacted and provided financial support to the tribes of Waziristan, headed by Hazi Mirza Khan, Fakir of Ipi. The Faqir's tribesmen had attacked British outposts at Waziristan and provided support for anti-allied propaganda activities in the North West Frontier Province (NWFP) presumably among the Indian nationalists who had fled into the area at the beginning of the war. Among those activists there were agents of Bose.

Through the Italians, the GIS contacted the Faqir of Ipi in the spring of 1941. The Germans hoped that Faqir could be used to unite and coordinate the activities of the various independent NWFP and Baluchistan tribes into a general uprising to coincide with other GIS activities in India. In preparation for the operation, which was given the name "FIRE-Eater" (Feuerfresser), Rahmat Khan took two w/t sets to the tribal region where he was to train three w/t operators.

Rahmat Khan also selected a secret site at an airfield where he stored several thousand gallons of RAF aviation gasoline stolen or bought on the black market, Hussein Zonober, Malik Mohammad Omar Khan, Ghulam Rahman, and Mira Jan were recruited locally to serve as support agents. All four were allegedly adherents of the Pir of Pagaro, leader of the Hur Muslim brotherhood.

The Faqir of Ipi continued to maintain contact with the Italians through a courier who came to Kabul, and the Italian Intelligence Service tried to maintain its advantageous position as the sole GIS channel to the Faqir. When the GIS learned that the Italians were claiming to be providing all the funds for the support of the Faqir -half of which was provided by the GIS -the GIS engineered direct contact with Abdul Rani, Faqir's agent in Kabul. The Faqir requested the German Legation in Kabul to intervene for the release of two of his agents, Afzal Khan, and Mir Sahib, who had been arrested by the Afghan police.

In November 1942, the Faqir of Ipi sent to Witzel, the GIS base chief in Kabul, a message advising that the Faqir had established contact with Hassan Khan, a tribal leader in Baluchistan. The courier who brought the message was accompanied by Ghul Habil, who on another matter was to contact the Afghan government for the Faqir, and who used the occasion to request more money from Anzilotti (chief of Italian operations in Kabul. At about the same time the Italian Intelligence Service's regular cut out with the Faqir, Waziri, a Royal Afghan Air Force Officer, was arrested in Kabul, possibly with gracious German "approval", leaving the GIS in possession of the only direct channel to the Faqir.

To achieve the necessary coordination of activities in the NWFP areas and other Indian centers Witzel tried to set up a liaison between the Fakir and the "M-Organization". In April 1943 Faqir reported that no "M-Organisation" couriers had yet arrived and he would, therefore, welcome European w/t operators to facilitate his operational contact with the GIS base at Kabul. GIS contact with Baluchistan tribal leader Hassan Khan was established in February

1942 using Subhan Khan as a cut-out. In August of that year, Subhan Khan was arrested by the Afghan police which not only endangered contact with Hassan Khan but also handicapped operations in India.

A GIS principal agent in India, Rahmat Khan alias Hantans-Lal alias Bhagat Ram was the main link between the GIS base in Kabul and the "M-Organization" intelligence network in India during World War II. He was one of the leaders of the "Forward Bloc" and a close collaborator of Subhas Chandra Bose. His brother reportedly was a member of the Indian parliament.

He held a leading position in the "M-Organization" as a member of the "Central Committee", and was fully trained in clandestine communications (s/w, encoding and decoding procedures, w/t, microfilm techniques) and sabotage. He was also an instructor of "M-Organization" agents in India, knew codes and signals used by "Azad Hind" a Berlin broadcast station, and in w/t traffic between "TIGER" (cryptonym for communications to or from the GIS base in Kabul) and "MARY" (the "M- Organization's" communications base in India). He was acquainted with many prominent Indian leaders and most of the GIS' Indian agents. At the beginning of World War II, he was in contact with the Italian Intelligence Service's base in Kabul but on the instructions of the GIS, he broke off contact with the Italians in December 1941.

In September 1943 per arrangements of the GIS, he contacted the Japanese Military Attache in Kabul to establish a new liaison with Subhas Chandra Bose after the latter departed for Japan. Soon thereafter (September-October 1943) the GIS discovered the RIS penetration of the "M-Organization" and concluded that Khan was a Soviet double agent.

Sodhi was a revolutionary nationalist leader and follower of Subhas Chandra Bose. In July 1940 he led the uprising in Bombay and

Central India and as a result, was sentenced to death in absentia. He fled to Waziristan, and in May 1941 went to Kabul, where he contacted the GIS base and made arrangements to travel to Germany. The trip was, however, cancelled for unknown reasons, and he returned to the North West Frontier Province where he became active in carrying out anti-British propaganda. He was said to be an expert in subversive propaganda among the Indian military. Reportedly he was also a member of an Indian revolutionary organization with headquarters in the USA, which, although allegedly non-Communist, had its representatives in Moscow.

In the summer of 1942, Sodhi was arrested by the British and allegedly subjected to third-degree interrogations during which he revealed the organizational structure of and GIS contacts in the "M-Organisation". Later in 1943, Subhas Chandra Bose called him a traitor.

The declassified CIA documents say, that in May 1943 Subhas Chandra Bose transferred to Tokyo, which caused further communication difficulties. In July 1943 the GIS agreed to put Rahmat Khan in touch with the Japanese Military Attached in Kabul, but as a result of several errors in tradecraft, the meeting never took place. Bose also made poor selections from among Japanese-trained agents who were sent to Inda via Burma, and who not only failed in their mission but also exposed several "M-Organization members to further compromise.

Despite this, in September 1943, when Japanese troops were fighting at the eastern approaches to India, the GIS at its Berlin headquarters worked out a new plan for a general uprising and the formation of a provisional government in India to coincide with the invasion of Indian soil proper by Japanese armed forces.At about the same time, however, GIS operations against India suffered two heavy blows. First, Capt Dietrich Witzel and his w/t operator Wilhelm Doh were expelled from Afghanistan.Secondly, Italy's surrender made exposure likely because the Italian Intelligence Service had extensive knowledge of GIS plans and operations in the area. As soon as Commercial AttacheRASMUSS -assumed the duties of the departing WITZEL, the RIS made known to penetration of the "M-Organization". Shortly thereafter RASMUSS was recalled to Germany and the Kabul base's activities ceased for all practical purposes. The Japanese Intelligence Service, through an agent, Tava Singh, purporting to be Subhas Bose's representative, attempted to continue contact with and guidance of the "M-Organization". Although the "M-Organization" operation was undoubtedly the most effective and extensive clandestine operation in India, it was not the only GIS effort.

From bases in the Far East, there were also GIS efforts aimed at "Target India." Presumably to counteract the increasing Japanese efforts against Indian nationalist leaders, the "Indian National Committee" was organized and hoped would unite all Indians in Japan. China, Thailand, and other Japanese-occupied territories. This group elected Swami Satyananda as chairman and Debnath Das as secretary but considered Subhas Bose as its principal chief.

In China, there was still another Indian nationalist group. the "Indian National Association", led by GIS-recruited A.M. Sahay. According to declassified CIA documents, the GIS base in Kabul maintained contact with several other persons on the Indo-Afghan border. In September 1942 these persons were listed as "YANIN", "YACUB", "BADAR", AMIU", "KHALEK", and "YUSSUF". In addition, a Moslem clerk at the British Legation in Kabul nicknamed "NEW OTTO", was in contact with one of the GIS agents from India.

It was reported from London on 14 February 1946 that the documents discovered by American intelligence officers prove beyond doubt that both Rashid Ali, former premier of Iraq, and Amin Hussaini, former Grand Mufti, both of whom were taking refuge in Saudi Arabia, were the chiefs of a gigantic espionage ring in the East. According to the weekly journal "Cavalcade", Subhas Chandra Bose was in charge of the Indian branch of that Eastern Espionage ring.

Declassified CIA documents provide an insight into the covert activities of the "M-Organization". Using organized tribal attacks against the British was part of Netaji Subhash Chandra Bose's strategy to enter British ruled India through the North-West Frontier and wage war against them. One radio message says that he would return to India in 1947. Eventually, there was a tribal revolt. Let us travel through the most complicated, thrilling, and shocking events.

CHAPTER THREE

The Faqir of Ipi in Waziristan

Waziristan, a barren hostile no-man's-land offering fertile soil on the border for embarrassing intrigues by Central Asian rivals of the British Empire, was still the main problem of British India's North-West Frontier. The chief hostile leader of this problem area was the notorious Faqir of Ipi.

Of medium height and on the lean side with a sparse beard, pale complexion, extremely reticent and by no means a soldier. His real name was Haji Mirza All Khan. He carried neither firearms nor a bandolier or daggers as other Waziris. He devoted most of his time to religious rites and ascetic ways of life. There is no definite record of his birth except that he was born in the village of Ipl within North Waziristan.

The Faqir came into the limelight in 1930 when he led a sympathetic movement in Waziristan, which was intended to support the North-West Frontier Congress movement of 1930-31. Though not a soldier himself, he collected about some experienced soldiers whose knowledge of strategy and tactics and whose leadership in guerilla warfare was unrivalled.

According to one account, the number of regular soldiers among his followers did not exceed 1,000, but his influence in Waziristan and the neighbouring areas was so great that he could muster large forces within a short time.

[The Fakir of Ipi]

On January 22, 1939, a small hamlet in the Kazha Valley, northern Waziristan, used by the Faqir of Ipi as a base from which he instigated raids on neighbouring districts was bombed from the air. In accordance with the authorities' usual precautions to avoid civilian loss of life, leaflets giving the villagers 24 hours warning to remove themselves and their families were dropped before the aircraft went into action. The Faqir had been harboured in the hamlet in defiance of Government orders and warnings.

[Attock Bridge on the River Indus, 1930]

German, Italian, and Japanese agents were believed to have been active in Afghanistan, several months before the Second World War broke out. The country was being used as a base for propaganda activities in the tribal areas.

By January 1941, Faqir was reportedly making contact with British Nazi agents in Afghanistan, and where there was a considerable German colony, the bombing was noticeable. A large number of pamphlets were being circulated in various parts of the country and some were filtering into the tribal areas adjoining the British Indian frontier.

"Nov. 15, 1946, Dinner Hotel Pierre, Pietro Quaroni. ... In 1933 Subhash Chandra Bose came to Rome and saw Mussolini. B. asked that some Italian officials be sent to India to keep in touch with their movement. That is when Q. first met B. in Rome. In 1930 Q. was sent to Kabul as Minister. ...After Bose was arrested by the British in Calcutta in 1939 his friends wrote to Q. in Kabul saying that B. wanted to go to Russia, Germany, and Italy, and asked for help. An Indian doctor who was a member of the Forward Bloc, but whom the British did not know as such, examined Bose in prison and reported that B. was too sick to stay in jail. He was released on parole, and plans were made for his escape. Q. arranged with Afghans to use tribesmen to get B. across the frontier. The tribesmen knew were friendly to him. The tribesmen used were Mohammadans. B. had grown a beard and moustache. He arrived in Kabul in February 1940 and stayed secretly in Q's house for more than a month until he left for Russia. ..."

Here B. is Subhas Chandra Bose and Q. is Pietro Quaroni, the Italian minister at Kabul, who supported King Amanullah and Bose in Afghanistan and India respectively against the British colonial power, was chiefly alleged to have driven Italian policy of involvement in the tribal frontier region.

In Afghanistan, the German Intelligence Service (GIS) worked feverishly, partly with the support of the Afghan Government, on penetrating Soviet and Indian territories. Turkmen emigres were used for intelligence missions into the Soviet Union. Support of some Indian tribal chieftains, such as the Faqir of Ipi, and control over a relatively strong extremist group in India was established and resulted in successful political riots and sabotage directed against the British. In addition, the GIS sponsored the anti-Bratish "M-Organization" and the "Indian National Army" for potential use in South Asia.

According to a German document released by the U.S. State Department, Germany, in 1941, planned to use Subhas Chandra Bose to spearhead an "extensive" propaganda campaign in the British Empire, promising that the Axis would liberate colonial people from British rule'.

The Faqir of Ipi in the North-West Frontier province area and the Grand Mufti of Jerusalem were also linked in the plan outlined by the German Foreign Minister, Von Ribbentrop.

Mussolini believed that the Faqir of Ipi and the Grand Mufti could be inducted to aid the Axis by the extensive use of money. He attached considerable importance to Grand Mufti's influence over the Arabs in a "holy war" against the British.

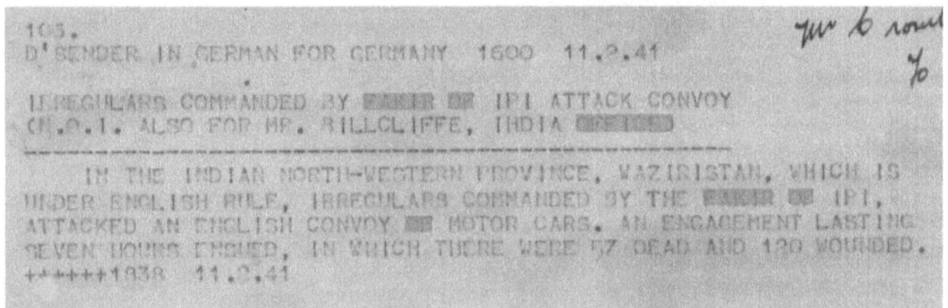

[Monitoring Intercept created: 7 Feb 1941- 15 Feb 1941]

Ribbentrop's intentions were revealed in a memorandum of the German foreign office covering a conversation between himself and Mussolini in Rome on May 13, 1941. Mussolini was much surprised to learn that Bose was in Germany and declared he agreed with the plan.

During the War, when the German and Italian nationals were rounded up in Persia and Afghanistan, some escaped into the hinterland and began a life of intrigue in disguise. A few of them reached Waziristan and placed their technical skill at the disposal of the Faqir of Ipi. It was said at that time that Faqir was maintaining direct wireless contact with Berlin and that even news of disturbances in India was convened to Berlin in this way.

The German technicians were said to have gone so far as to prepare a landing ground near Ipi's headquarters for supply aircraft that would bring ammunition from Germany for the Faqir's forces which were to strike simultaneously with the entry of the German forces into Persia.

The Faqir had a plentiful supply of arms and ammunition and by means of levying these, built up his stocks wherever he moved his headquarters in Waziristan. During the war, his guerilla fighters were using Italian cartridges and German hand grenades. His followers often managed to draw British troops into convenient traps which necessitated long lines of communication. Convoys moving around these extended routes with provisions, arms, and ammunition intended for the troops were attacked and seized.

Waziris generally took every opportunity of seizing anything they could get from the Army. While their primary object was always supplies, they occasionally took hostages against the detention of their comrades or the punishment of those who helped them. They believed that Faqir had supernatural powers.

It is indisputable that the Faqir was the supreme authority in the Waziri uplands. His word was law among the tribesmen and not even the "friendly" of them could safely disobey his orders.

It was reported in February 1946 that Italy was in contact with the Faqir of Ipi and was attempting by using large sums of money to get him, as well as the Mufti, to carry on some activity. There was every reason to believe that Faqir Ipi had a hand in the kidnapping of Major J. O. S. Donald, a British political agent. By the end of July, Faqir of Ipi was reported to have received a large sum of money from abroad through agents in Kabul.

[British military crossing the Tochi River, travelling to Bannu]

It was reported in September 1946 that Netaji was the guest of Faqir of Ipi where Faqir had placed all his resources and men at his disposal. Newspaper alleged that the motive behind the bombing of Waziristan was apparently to kill Netaji but he was hale and hearty despite the bombing operations.

Indian Foreign Policy was a new element in world affairs... travelling to the Frontier region in person and meeting both Abdul Gaffar Khan -nominally a Congress ally and the Faqir of Ipi -who sometimes said, was a Muslim League ally.

As Pandit Nehru's plane landed at Razmak, Nehru heard drums of revolt. Faqir of Ipi was being sought in his cave fastness of the Afghan border delegation of frontier Congress supporters.

After the bombing of the North-West Frontier, punishing the tribesmen appeared in both the British and Indian Press. The Faqir of Ipi had been taking a leading part in preparing a welcome for

Pandit Nehru. Faqir declared himself in favour of achieving definite independence over large areas of the border regions and closer contact with the Afghans.

In October 1946 Faqir of Ipi was reported as ready to come to Terms. "We cannot expect any help from League," Khan Mahomed Yunus Khan said in Peshawar that he had received three letters, including one from the Faqir of Ipi himself.Indian Government had no desire to carry on a feud with anybody and would welcome friendly relations with the Faqir of Ipi, said Shri Jagjivan Ram, Labour Member.

The Faqir of Manki Sharif and his party, who had been sent by the British Resident in Waziristan to spread Muslim League propaganda, were ignored by the Faqir of Ipi. Reported promise by Faqir of Ipi to Manki Pir to help in founding free Islamic State -briefly relating the story of his tour in Waziristan, the Pir Sahib of Manki Sharif, who was the first Muslim League leader to tour Waziristan.

Speculation was rife in informed quarters in New Delhi regarding Khan Abdul Ghaffar Khan's visit to Mountbatten in the company of Gandhiji in April 1947. It was reported that Ghaffar Khan had serious allegations against the Political Department in the Frontier Province, allegedly responsible firstly, for the attack during Pandit Nehru's Frontier tour and secondly, for the present League agitation and communal disturbances in the Frontier Province.

Ghaffar Khan, brother of the Frontier Premier, Doctor Khan Saheb, said a lot to tell Mountbatten of the Frontier's complicated politics and alleged official-sponsored reactionary intrigues against the Congress Government, and of official mismanagement of tribal and border affairs, for complicating the administrative communal political problems during the transfer of power to Indian hands.

It was reported from Peshawar that general directives to tribesmen regarding the attitude they should adopt towards the future India Government had been given by the Faqir of Ipi in a poster, thousands of copies of which were distributed in the tribal areas.

The poster said: "Of late we have come to know that Congress has gained strength to such an extent that it can make the British quit the sacred soil of Hindustan force and Waziristan, and therefore it wants to negotiate terms of mutual interest and welfare of the settled and tribal areas.

"If that is so, we are ready to come to terms with the accredited ambassadors of India because we feel without such an arrangement no agreement could be really binding.

"We have been deceived by cunning British diplomacy in season and out of season and we cannot now afford to fall prey to any more hypocrisy and cheating. Right from the beginning we have been crusading against the British Government for the maintenance of our religious rights and economic and political freedom.

"Whosoever favours our programme on the above lines can befriend us with pleasure. We harbour no ill will towards any Indian. The real enemy of us all is the British who are responsible for creating suspicion and distrust between the two great peoples of Hindustan and Waziristan.

"As such it is our bounden duty to refuse the British any assistance in their underhand games." The followers were ever ready to heed the call to war of men like the Faqir of IPi, the Haji of Turangzai, and the Faqir of Allmon, even if the new series of raids on the highway of danger was imminent.

In spite of the declaration in the Press that the Faqir of Ipi was a supporter of the Muslim League's claim for an independent state of Pakistan in Northwest and Northeast India, it was learnt on good authority that the Faqir continued on his non-committal course as regards Indian politics. He was a friend neither of the Congress nor the Muslim League.

In May 1947, the Faqir of Ipi who for twelve years had been waging a "holy war" against the British in Waziristan on the North-West Frontier of India, offered to mediate between Congress and the Muslim League. In a poster, which he had circulated widely,

Faqir said, "Representatives of both sides have approached us for support but as I don't know the actual position, I refrained from interfering. But I am prepared to work for an amicable settlement if both parties accept me as mediator." Did Faqir conciliate Congress and the Muslim League, the two main political parties?

Faqir of Ipi was reportedly behind the raids from North-West Frontier and India's North-West tribesmen were again on the rampage. In October 1947, the Pakistan Government decided to give unconditional pardon to the Faqir of Ipi and allow him to settle in any part of Pakistan he liked. His followers would also be dealt with leniently.

On June 21, 1947, Pashtun nationalists organized a jirga in the Bannu district of what is today Khyber Pakhtunkhwa (then NWFP) to decide the future of Pashtuns. The jirga favoured an independent state of Pashtunistan. The Faqir of Ipi strongly supported the jirga and the Pashtunistan declaration.

In July, a four-man delegation of Red Shirts who met the Faqir of Ipi returned to Bannu. One member interviewed said, that Faqir of Ipi was in favour of the Frontier Congressmen's decision to boycott the coming referendum and that he had advised the Pathans to abstain from voting.

Faqir's guerrilla policy continued after the establishment of Pakistan in August 1947. The tribal lashkars called the establishment of Pakistan the continuation of British imperialism.

Speaking from the Pakistan broadcasting station, Peshawar the Frontier Premier warned all supporters of Pathanistan who were in League with enemies of Pakistan that they would be treated as enemies of the Muslim nation.

Khan Abdul Quyam Khan said some Red Shirts would have us believe that Pathanistan was only a cry for autonomy within the framework of the Dominion of Pakistan. "We heard this and thought that better counsels had started to prevail but we have since found to our dismay that believers in Pathanistan are in League with enemies of Pakistan and that they are secretly carrying on activities which we cannot tolerate at all. Let me again warn that we look upon them as enemies of Pakistan and that we propose to treat them accordingly. Let them remember that only one flag can fly in this country and that flag is the flag of Pakistan."

In January 1948, Faqir the incrowned lord of Waziristan was reported to be lying seriously ill in his mountain retreat. In the next month, Ghaffar Khan cleared the misunderstanding about his Pathanistan Idea, envisaged by him as an autonomous area within the framework of Pakistan. Red Shirt leader repudiated the suggestions that the Faqir of Ipi was in any way connected with the Pathanistan movement.

After watching Ghaffar Khan's activities for more than nine months it was alleged that he was on his way to meet agents of the Faqir of Ipi who in the past had been identified with frontier disturbances, "with a view to stirring up trouble in the border."

Steps were to be taken to deal with Pakistan's enemies in N.W.F.P., but after his visit to Karachi, he had again started his anti-Pakistan activities. In his reference to the Faqir of Ipi, the Frontier Premier said that the Faqir was prepared to wage war against the British.

It was learnt in Lahore that Sirdar Habibullah Khan, Torkhel Wazir, nephew of the Faqir of Ipi, sent the following telegram to Pandit Jawahar Lal Nehru -"The tribal people are keenly watching your tactics..."

In June 1948,a copy of a letter from the Faqir of Ipi promising to join India in an attack on Pakistan in return for financial assistance appeared in the Karachi newspaper "Dawn." The letter was alleged to be found in the possession of Awwal Husain, a 35-year-old Pathan, who admitted when arrested by Pakistan police that he was an agent of the Faqir.

Soon, fifty gunmen, followers of the Faqir of Ipi were reportedly killed in a clash with Pakistan police at Bannu in the North-West Frontier Province, adjoining Waziristan. Officials at Peshawar said the Faqir had denounced Pakistan as a British colony and ordered his followers to wage war against the country.

Within the next seven days, it was reported that the planes of the Royal Pakistan Air Force were used to put down the trouble on the North East Frontier stirred up by the tribal followers of Faqir. There were only small skirmishes and all was quiet now.

The Faqir was now accused by Khan Abdul Quayyum Khan, North-West Frontier Province Premier, of having agreed to act as an agent for the Hindu in return for a few pieces of silver.

His village was surrounded, the Frontier Province Government announced, and 31 members of his gangs were captured. This followed the arrest of Abdul Gaffar Khan, the former Congress "Red Shirt" leader, who was jailed the next day for three years. The Frontier Government said he was on his way to meet agents of the Faqir to stir up trouble on the border.

Pakistan would be ruthlessly stamped out. He deplored the anti-Pakistan activities of Khan Abdul Ghaffar Khan, and the Faqir of Ipi and said that both of them were deliberately playing into the hands of enemies of the State. The Pakistan Government was its enemy and for this reason, they were constantly endeavouring to enlist foreign aid. The Faqir of Ipi had been trying to obtain assurances of help from Nehru.

In the next month, the Faqir of Ipi attacked a Pakistan post with a Lashkar and retreated in disorder the very day his accomplice Abdul Ghaffar Khan was arrested. Ipi had struck rather a sticky patch. While Indian forces drew uncomfortably close to its frontiers of Kashmir, the Faqir of Ipi had been giving considerable trouble in the North, and Sind was growing sulky in the South.

The Faqir of Ipi had been appealing for assistance to Kabul. Sardar Shah Wali Khan. It was reported in August that Faqir was arrested by the Pakistan Government on charges of treason and conspiracy. The Pakistan Government claimed that it had proof to show that India in collaboration with the Faqir of Ipi was going to attack Pakistan. They alleged that documentary evidence revealed plans for a joint summer offensive by India and the Faqir of Ipi against Pakistan.

In 1948, Faqir took control of Datta Khel and moved toward the establishment of an independent state of Pashtunistan. In this regard, he established strong ties with regional political leaders. By the end of February 1949, reports were reaching Karachi that the Faqir of Ipi had become active again and resumed hostile activities against Pakistan. It was reported in March, Pakistan general headquarters announced in Karachi that Faqir of Ipi lost 50 men in an attack with mortar and light machine guns on Thal Fort, in Pakistan territory.

A Pakistan army spokesman announced at Rawalpindi, West Punjab that the Faqir attacked the fortress of Thal on the borders of Afghanistan. Six hundred of his raiding tribesmen were beaten off with mortar and machinegun fire. Armed North-West Frontier constabulary holding the fortress suffered no casualties.

CIA declassified report dated 27 April 1949 says: "The Faqir of Ipi had been in regular contact with the Russian Embassy in Kabul using tribesmen couriers. It could be speculated that the Afghanistan government was well aware of what was going on. During one of the skirmishes in North Waziristan, Pakistan Tochi scout captured for the first time, an Afghan Army officer. The officer was dressed as a tribesman."

In May 1949, the Faqir of Ipi called on a tribal jirga in Gurwek, North Waziristan, and asked Pakistan to accept Pashtunistan as an independent state. To counter his lashkars, Pakistan favoured bombing his safe havens to undermine the tribal revolt. In 1953-54, No. 14 Squadron of the Pakistan Air Force led an operation from Miranshah airbase and heavily bombarded the Faqir of Ipi's compound.

In June, some planes were on reconnaissance over the Pakistan side of the North-West Frontier when they saw a strong concentration of Faqir's followers accompanied by a contingent of Afghan levies. In the next month, the firebrand Faqir quit his hide-out.

In the next year, he was active among frontier personalities and was advocating Pukhtoonistan. At one time liaison was maintained between the Indian Government and the Faqir of Ipi with the obvious purpose of counter-damaging Pakistan. But since then the Faqir seemed to lose influence.

In August 1951, it was reported that the Afghan envoy in the UK criticised the arranged Pakhtoonistan Day: loyalty of Pakistani tribesmen on their side of the Durand Line. Apart from the Government of Afghanistan, the Faqir of Ipi was one of the shining lights of this stunt. The fact that the Durand Line constitutes the international boundary limits.

Despite the use of mighty force, the Faqir of Ipi had never surrendered and eventually died of an illness on April 16, 1960.

CHAPTER FOUR

American Correspondent Says Bose Is Alive

In an exclusive report to the "National Call," Mr. Alfred Wagg, the famous American correspondent, reveals certain completely new facts to scotch the theory of the death of Netaji Bose and to support the idea which has been gaining ground in several well-informed quarters that Netaji is still alive and is about them expected to reappear on the political scene at the psychological moment.

Mr. Wagg furnishes conclusive evidence to prove that there was no air crash for several months before or after the time when it is alleged Netaji's plane crashed at Taihoku as stated in the official Japanese statement. If there was no air crash at Taihoku the official Japanese statement clearly cannot be relied upon as conclusive. Mr. Wagg further reveals the fact that Subhas Chandra Bose according to one informant was seen in the company of a Chinese General known to him, several months after his official death in the air crash.

Alfred Wagg writes:

The Home Minister's announcement that all charges against Mr Subhas Chandra Bose are now withdrawn by the Interim Government comes as no surprise to those of us who believe that Bose is still alive.

No one today is prepared to say "where I saw Bose and when" but as a member of the American Press who has consistently written on Bose in American and the Indian Press, I feel now I can reveal my private and personal reasons for the fall of believing that Bose is alive and is about to launch a political campaign inside India with far-reaching social and economic results which will most likely be inaugurated. I am told, with a huge rally "somewhere in Central India" to be entitled the "Bose Conference of Friends."

To the Conference of Friends is expected every major political representation. I have been told by Jai Prakash Narain that if such a conference does materialise, he will attend on certain conditions.

The Muslim High Command has said that they wish to attend and further stated to me that they feel that a coalition is possible with Bose. Others place various faiths and feelings pro and con.

For these reasons lending extreme and immediate importance to the return of Bose as a man who might or might not unite India, here is the story of my interest as an observer and a foreign press man.

I first doubted the story of Netaji Bose's death when in French Indo-China just after the war **I was told thatten days after the supposed crash in Taihoku Formosa, Bose attended a meeting in Saigon.** By the sight of pictures, I accepted this evidence as fact or at least sufficient reason to seriously doubt the Japanese story. Since then much evidence has come on in both sides, and as the public become more frustrated with conflicting stories, I became more interested in ascertaining whether Bose was dead or alive.

Conflicting Facts:

From the intelligence reports received in America and elsewhere which were reported to me I was told during the winter of 1945 that Bose was alive. Further, I learnt last spring that Bose had been seen in company with a Chinese General (also known to me) on April 28. On the May 23, I arrived in New Delhi from America by plane. I was then told that my story could not be true because Colonel Rahman of the LN.A. had been on the spot at Taihoku,

Formosa when Netaji died at Taihoku from burns as a result of an air crash. To prove this story and disprove my theory four pictures were produced to show the scene and plane crash in Taihoku where Netaji met death.

No Crash At Taihoku:

I viewed the pictures with extreme care and great interest. The result of this interest led me to interview two officers who were prisoners of war and who had been on the airfield in question all during August when the crash was supposed to have taken place.

They took oath that the background in the pictures was not that of Taihoku, that there were no railroad tracks on or near the airfield as shown in the pictures, that there were no large rocks on the airfield as shown in the pictures, and, finally, that whether the pictures were faked or not, there was no crash at Taihoku for over six months place.

The Champagne Road:

But this evidence alone did not satisfy my curiosity. For at the same time, the French were mysteriously jumping their paratroops in an area of Siam which is of little value to them or the Siamese and of no consequence of the French Indo-China-Siam border dispute. Here a semi-secret smugglers highway known as the "The Champagne Road," which is a mere widened footpath, connects French Indo-China with India and Burma through Siam.

With these French paratroops were reported by the Siamese to be British uniformed observers. After some weeks of investigation, I was told (whether true or not I cannot vouch for) that this was another effort to trap Bose.

Death Not Proven:

Then letters began to arrive from an old friend who always knew Bose. In these letters were Bose's theories which I presume Netaji Bose wishes to explain himself if he is still alive. I do not claim that the evidence that has fallen into my hands during these journalistic investigations, which I undertook purely through professional interests conclusively proves Netaji Subhas Chandra Bose is alive but, it does show that all the facts hitherto put forward publicly to support the theory of his death are inconclusive, based on defective evidence and in several cases seem to be false. I leave those equally interested in this subject, therefore, to draw their own conclusions."

The Story Of Netaji's Air-Crash In Formosa Is A Myth!

The story of Netaji Subhas Chandra Bose's death in an air crash in Taihoku on Formosa island is a myth, according to this on the spot enquiry of Mr. Wagg. He reported the results of his enquiry to India's Prime Minister, Sri Jawaharlal Nehru. Much later in June 1951, giving his reactions to the reported move for bringing to India what was described to be Netaji's ashes from Tokyo, Sri Amiya Nath Bose, nephew of Netaji disclosed that he came to know about the on the spot enquiry from Prime Minister Sri Jawaharlal Nehru himself.

CHAPTER FIVE

Nehru Does Not Believe Netaji Is Alive

An American journalist of Chicago Tribune, Alfred Wag, told Pandit Nehru on August 29, 1945, in Delhi that after the Japanese broadcast, 'Bose was alive and seen 4 days ago in Saigon. On Sept 11, 1945, Nehru himself told API at Jhansi, 'Like many other people, he did not believe the story about the reported death of Subhas Chandra Bose... I have received a number of reports, which have raised me in great doubt and I disbelieve the authenticity of the news [Declassified PMO Political File: 871/11/P/16/92 Pol].

But on 12 October 1946, Amrita Bazar Patrika reported that 'Nehru Does Not Believe Netaji is Alive. It reads: "Pandit Jawaharlal Nehru in a statement today expressed his conviction, based on a letter received by him from Colonel Habibur Rahman, that all rumours suggesting that Mr. Subhas Chandra Bose is alive, are without foundation.

Pandit Nehru's statement was: From time to time some item of news appears in the Press relating to Netaji Subhas Chandra Bose. It is stated that he is alive, that he is coming to India soon, that he has been seen in some part of India, that somebody has received a message from him, and so on and so forth. Sometimes even a date is fixed for his public appearance in India. When closely examined, these items of news turn out to be just rumours or vague hopes. But this constant repetition of this theme has undoubtedly made many people believe that Shri Subhas Chandra Bose is alive. I do not think there is the slightest justification for this belief.

For some months after the news of his death came, I was rather doubtful of its veracity. Later, when Colonel Habibur Rahman gave me a detailed eye-witness account of the accident which resulted in the death, I became convinced of it. No piece of news has come to me since then or has appeared in the Press, that has shaken that conviction. All of us would like him to be alive, but it is no good feeding ourselves with rumour which is without foundation.

But very soon, the Interim Government said that there was "No News" regarding Netaji Bose. On October 30, Home Minister Sardar Patel replied to a question in the Central Assembly: 'The Indian Government is not in a position to make any authoritative statement as to whether Netaji Subhas Chandra Bose is dead or alive. Sardar Patel added that Pandit Nehru's recent statement on the subject was not an official opinion.

But the legend that Subhas Bose was alive was growing daily and the younger generation had been rallying to shadow-rival of the aged Mahatma. Such was the hold of Subhas Chandra Bose on the masses at that time.

DEAD MAN "RISES"

★ ★ ★

Shadow-rival threatens Ghandi's power

[The Leader-Post: 08 January, 1946]

Prof. Samar Guha, in his book *Netaji- Dead or Alive?* [pp 277] raises the most relevant question: Subhas Bose, in the days of

Tripuri crisis in 1939 depicted Pandit Nehru in a letter addressed to him, as like his 'elder brother'. But what this elder brother did about Netaji? British Government decided "to leave Bose where he was" -Nehru faithfully followed the same policy, a policy of greatest betrayal of the greatest hero of Indian national freedom. Since his return from Singapore after meeting Mountbatten there in 1946, Nehru never uttered a word, of his own, about Netaji since he came to power.

In his *Unsolved mystery* [The Statesman, Jan 23, 1992], Prof. Samar Guha writes: Even after the Red Fort Trial of INA men in 1946, he (Gandhiji) told Colonel Habibur Rahaman: "Habib whatever you may tell me to the contrary, I still believe in my heart of hearts that Netaji Subhas Chandra Bose is alive."

On October 18, 1946, The Indian Daily Mail's (Singapore) leader criticising Pandit Nehru's statement on Netaji's death as hasty and ill-advised received wide publicity in the Indian Press.Similar views were expressed by Mr. Saojee, a prominent Congressman from the Central Provinces, who says:Pandit Nehru's statement contains nothing new.**Subhas Chandra Bose is alive but not in India.** "Arrangements are being made to bring him into India by his trusted Forward Bloc colleagues all this is strong ground to hope that Netaji will be back soon."

Several committees had been set up by the Government of India to probe into the matter of the 'Plane-Crash'. Colonel Habibur Rahman stood by his theory of Netaji's death, even though he couldn't convince the British and American investigation teams or any of his INA colleagues. The British investigation team interrogated Habibur Rahman and found out that Rahman was unwilling to come out with the truth. It is believed that his version is that of a soldier's statement in defence of the escape plan of his master.

Prof. Samar Guha, again in his book *Netaji- Dead or Alive?* [pp 154] brilliantly analyses: 'Ishoda, Hachia and Negishi, Iyer, Pritam Singh, Gulzara Singh, Hasan, and Debnath Das, -all either former ministers of Netaji's Government or top-ranking INA and Japanese officers told Shah Nawaj Committee and Khosla Commission almost similar stories about the happenings at Saigon. Their story was almost identical, but it totally differed from the story of Habibur Rahaman. Thus Rahaman gave out a fourth package of lies to the British Team.'

Habibur Rahman showed a rectangular watch with a burnt band saying that Netaji had it on his wrist when he was engulfed in the burning flame after the air crash. But it was known to every personnel that Netaji always used a round-shaped wristwatch and not any rectangular one. When INA Defense Committee Chief Bhulabhai Desai asked Habibur Rahman to open the watch, he found that the oil inside the watch was intact, although Habibur Rahman claimed that it was almost consumed in flame at the time of the air crash. Shri Desai smiled and returned the watch to Rahman without saying a word.

While describing the air crash, Habibur Rahman used to say that when the plane crashed he was wearing a woolen jumper, whereas Netaji wore a Khaki suit on his body. He was asked how it was possible that not a single thread of his inflammable woolen jumper was burnt but Netaji's fireproof clothes caught fire "horribly"? Habibur fumbled to answer the question.

Again, Habibur said that he made a frantic effort with both his hands to put out the flame all around Netaji's body after the air crash. But when he was asked how could it happen that the palms of his two hands bore no burnt marks whereas the dorsal of his two hands showed some hazy marks, which in all probability could be of acid-burn? He looked confused and didn't try to explain.

"In 1947 before he moved to Pakistan, Habibur Rahman lived with his father-in-law who was the 'Prime Minister' of the Princely State of Alwar. He confessed to Mr. Khemchand, the CS Secretary to the Alwar Prime Minister that Netaji's death story was nothing but cooked up.

It was reported by the Indian Daily Mail dated 18 September 1951, that despite Col. Habibur Rahman's testimony, there were countless reports of Subhas Chandra Bose still alive. India's Deputy

Foreign Minister, Dr. B.V. Keskar, told questioners in Parliament, **"the government of India is not in a position to give irrefutable proof of his death."**

"There is no doubt, said one prominent Indian leader, "that if Bose should reappear today he would challenge Pandit Nehru as a national leader". "He led the only army to invade India in modern times, built by the Japanese from British Indian forces captured in the fall of Singapore and elsewhere in East Asia. Bose urged direct and bloody action to throw out British rule from India, called Gandhi approach "his appeasement with the evil. Yet millions of Indians continue to regard him as their saint and leader."

But again on March 5, 1952, Jawahar Lal Nehru replied in Parliament to Mr. H.V. Kamath -"I have no doubt in my mind. I did not have it then and I have no doubt today that the question of Netaji Subhas Chandra Bose's death, I think is settled beyond doubt. There can be no inquiry about that." [Declassified PMO Political File: 800/6/C/3/88-Pol].

Mr. Kamath asked: "Is it not a fact that on several occasions in the House the late Sardar Patel and Dr. Keskar stated thgat they had no irrefutable evidence or proof of the death of Netaji?"

On the report submitted by Mr. S.A. Ayer on the air-crash and death of Bose at Taihoku, Pandit Nehru replied: "This is the fullest and latest account of the air crash we have had. Whether it is the last word or not, I cannot say. It does seem to me that it is a fairly convincing account."

In 1956, Habibur Rahman came to Delhi from Pakistan to appear before the Shah Nawaz Committee. However, a few days before his departure for Delhi the 'Civil and Military Gazette' of Lahore published a news that Habibur Rahman told this paper that **Netaji didn't die in the air crash**. This report was published in 'East Pakistan' dailies also. But **he declined to contradict it**. Habibur Rahman refused to appear before Khosla Commission to avoid cross examination by the judicial commission. Before non-judicial Shah Nawaz Committee he submitted just a written statement.

Rumours that Subhash Chandra Bose was alive and waiting to make a "big comeback" are some of the concerns about India in the US that have been revealed in documents dating back to the 1950s declassified by the Central Intelligence Agency (CIA) under the Freedom of Information Act:

US lost sleep over Soviets planting Bose imposter

"There is another political note... it may have some real potential danger in it. I was impressed on many occasions by the fact that Subhash Chandra Bose... is still a very popular hero. This expression of great enthusiasm clearly indicated to me that Bose is a National Hero, and in the eyes of the man on the street, I think he ranks next to Ghandi (SIC).

It is now rumoured that... he is alive... waiting for a chance to make a big comeback. Officially, Bose was declared 'lost' when the ship he was on was sunk en route from Buram to Japan. Whether Bose is dead or alive is relatively unimportant but the possibility of an imposter should not be overlooked. I have had several educated Indians tell me that the USSR would send an imposter for Bose into India and it would be easy to convince the people that he is Bose. If Bose or an imposter should return, it is probable that a great many of the people would accept his leadership."

I think that Nehru wants both Soviet friendship and US money and to obtain both, he is trying to play both ends against the middle. ..." [The Times of India, 30 Nov 2009].

In a personal letter to Shri Suresh Chandra Bose, elder brother of Subhas Chandra Bose, Nehru writes: "I have your letter of the 12th May 1962, You ask me to send you the proof of the death of Netaji Subhas Chandra Bose, **I cannot send you any precise and direct proof.** After a lapse of time now, there is extreme probability of his being alive somewhere secretly." This letter was dated 13th May 1962. Even seventeen years after the so-called air-crash and six years after the conclusion of the Shah Nawaz Committee of Enquiry, which officially declared Netaji dead, Nehru himself could not be sure about being in a position to supply incontrovertible proof of Netaji's death!

In 1964 CIA thought Subhash Chandra Bose was alive [HT]: In February 1964, the CIA interviewed a former agent of the British Counter Intelligence Corps, whose name is censored in the declassified documents and who suggested Bose could have been alive in 1964.

"There now exists a strong possibility that Bose is leading a religious group undermining the current (Jawaharlal) Nehru government," the CIA had said.

Shri Amiya Nath Bose, nephew of Subhas Bose, in his letter dated April 20, 1964, demanded: "...that there should be an official judicial finding regarding the air-crash at Taihuku and that the Chief Justice of India may be requested to preside over a body of judges to enquire into the question."

In his reply dated April 22, 1964, Panditji stated: "**I agree with you that something should be done to finalise this question of Netaji's death.** But it is not quite clear to me how far it will be proper for me to ask the Chief Justice of India to look into the matter. It may involve visiting Japan, and I am sure I cannot ask the Chief Justice to do so."

In August 1964, Shri Amiya Nath Bose invited late P.M. Shri Shastri's attention to the aforesaid correspondence with Panditji and reiterated his demand for a judicial inquiry. India's first prime minister, who had differed with Bose, died in May 1964.

Declassified PMO Poltical File: 870/11/P/17/90 reveals: Professor Samar Guha, Ex-M.P. (Lok Sabha), writes in his letter dated 5th November, 1988 to Mekhail Gorbachev, the then Presidenrt of USSR.: 'During the early part of 1946, a secret report sent to the British Viceroy in India by its intelligence stated: "There is a secret report which says, Nehru received a letter from Bose saying that he was in Russia and wanted to escape to India." Did not Nehru know what happened to Bose?

Rajesh Talwar in his article, 'Nehru and the Netaji mystery' [The Daily Guardian; 23 January, 2021], argues: "he knew perfectly well that there had been no air crash in Taipei. It was for this reason that he forbade the Shah Nawaz Commission from travelling to Taiwan on the specious ground that this could affect relations with China. ...It was moreover not something inconsequential that he was hiding, but a powerful secret the disclosure of which would have major international consequences. The question really should be: was Nehru hiding things in general public interest or in his own interest.

...Nehru kept Bose's family under surveillance for decades. The fear that the truth about Bose would somehow come to light haunted him so much that he even set the Indian Embassy to spy on Bose's nephew while he was travelling in Japan. If Nehru went to so far as to enquire as to whether the Bose nephew went to the Temple, he had certainly something to hide -a terrible, dark secret."

CHAPTER SIX

1946: Netaji Subhas Chandra Bose In Frontier

On September 2, 1945, World War II ended when U.S. General Douglas MacArthur accepted Japan's formal surrender aboard the U.S. battleship Missouri, anchored in Tokyo Bay along with a flotilla of more than 250 Allied warships. Surprisingly even in December 1945 and January 1946, British intelligence was curious about how Netaji Subhas Chandra Bose went to Japan from India. The declassified documents reveal that the Deputy Inspector General of Police, C.I.S., Bombay Province was sending SECRET letters on the subject to the Assistant Director (W), I.B., H.D., Govt of India, New Delhi.

In one such communique, he sent a translation of an article regarding Subhas Chandra Bose's escape that appeared in the "Dainik Samachar" of December 20, 1945:

'The North-West Frontier Province has very often in the past proved important in Indian History. Several times the famous British Army suffered defeat at the hands of tribes who inhabit the country. But today a little incident has brought this Province once again in the limelight. This is due to its connection with the disappearance of Subhas Chandra Bose from his house in Calcutta.

Mr. R.K. Karanjia, the representative of a newspaper who is touring the country, has published the following story. In this, he appears to have used information from documents with the Government of India. The whole world considers Subhas Chandra

Bose's escape from India as one of the greatest riddles of World War II.

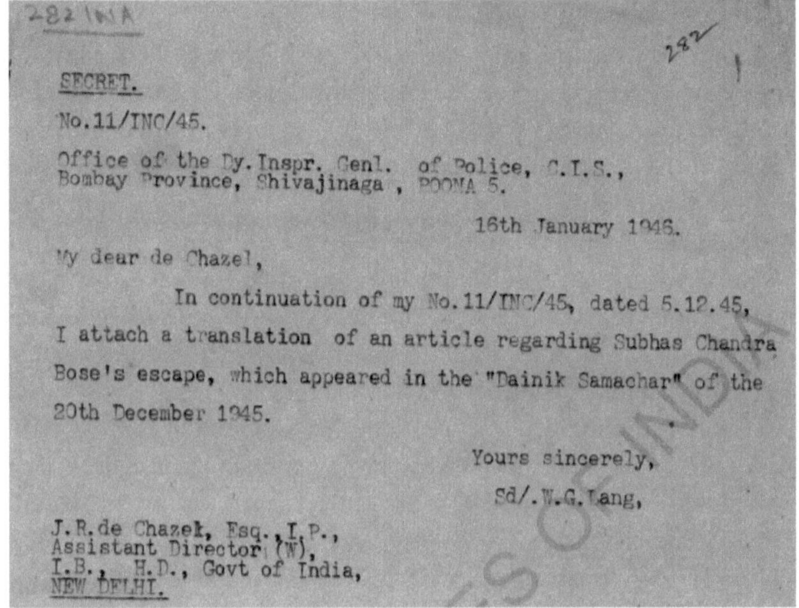

[Declassified File 282/INA]

Mr. Karanjia describes the N.W.F.P. as a beautiful but dangerous country. Many of the links in the route for Bose's escape from India in 1939 are to be found in this Province. He says that in spite of the time that has elapsed since the incident, he is able to obtain and send information of this mysterious incident.

First to Russia and then to Germany. Current public opinion on S.C. Bose's escape is that he sailed for Japan on a Japanese ship from the Bay of Bengal. This is incorrect. S.C. Bose went first to Kabul via Peshawar, through the Khyber Pass, and then went to Russia and Germany. The Indian Frontier can be crossed only at two points in the N.W.F.P. One route enters Afghanistan and the other leads to Russia. Two methods are open for doing this: to obtain permission from the British authorities or to bribe a passage from the hill tribes. In the latter case, the hill tribes guarantee safe escorts across the frontier on money being paid.

Naturally, S.C. Bose employed the second means. Evidence of S.C. Bose having been last seen in this locality is available at Sub Kadar a hill outpost. Subhas Chandra Bose's disappearance came to the notice of the secret police a month after his escape when enquiries were initiated. This month's interval afforded S.C. Bose sufficient time to make complete arrangements for leaving India. ...'

But that's not all. Bose planned to do another Imphal through the North-West Frontier Province. There are multiple reports on Bose's presence in the N.W.F.P in 1946, much later than the news of his 'death' in a plane crash went into circulation.

The Allied intelligence force didn't have an inkling of what Bose was going to do next. Bose's outstanding courage, foresightedness, unparallel leadership, and charismatic presence on the battlefield terrified the British.

'In the early hours of February 26th, 1945, Netaji stood at the foot of Mount Popa in Burma. Every now and then there was a flash of gunfire or the blaze of a bomb on the north-western horizon. The sky seemed full of enemy planes whose pilots were briefed - "Look for Bose- the notorious INA head, Japanese puppet, and traitor. Kill him."

Considering it a very insignificant danger, Netaji scorned -"England has not made a bomb that can kill me.", writes Dr. Satyanarayan Sinha in his book *Netaji Mystery*.

Such was the fear of Netaji Subhash Chandra Bose in their mind that Mr. R.F. Mudie the then Home Minister in the Viceroy's Executive Council, while replying to Mr. E.M. Jenkin's letter -Top secret No. 1157 dated August 11, 1945, regarding "Disposal of Bose" finally suggested (P 107, VOL VI):- **"Leave him where he is and don't ask for his surrender or release"**, adding, **"he might, of course, in certain circumstances, be welcomed by the Russian".**

A Central Intelligence Department's confidential report was that **Subhas Bose was in the Soviet Union under the assumed name of "GIZAI MILAN"** a fact disclosed by the top Russian diplomats in Afghanistan and Iran. [Source: Declassified SECRET PMO Political File No. 800/6/C/3/88 -Pol]

S Section CSDIC (I), SEAC SECRET report to HQ Fourteenth Army, GSI (b) on October 20, 1945

THE PRESENT ACTIVITIES OF S.C. BOSE

N.R.S. NAIDU, 99 Sophia Rd. Responsible for the report that he heard a Moscow broadcast denying BOSE's death. The broadcast went on to say that **BOSE would do another Imphal from the west of India.**

THE PRESENT ACTIVITIES OF S.C. BOSE.

23.   N.R.S. NAIDU, 99 Sophia Rd.   Responsible for the report that he heard a Moscow broadcast denying BOSE's death.   The broadcast went on to say that BOSE would do another Imphal from the west of India.

[Declassified File No. 75/INA/National Archives of India]

It was reported on December 14, 1945, by Civil & Military Gazette (Lahore) that "An interesting disclosure that **Mr. Subhas Chandra Bose, Netaji of Azad Hind Army had escaped through the frontier and had also visited all important places of pilgrimage of all religions, including Lakshmi Narayan temple,** has been made by a soldier of the Indian National Army, recently released from confinement, when he interviewed Pandit Prem Prakash Daveshar in the Durgiana temple."

MR. SUBHAS CHANDRA BOSE'S ESCAPE

(From Our Own Correspondent)

AMRITSAR, Dec. 13.—An interesting disclosure that Mr. Subhas Chandra Bose, Netaji of Azad Hind Army had escaped through the frontier and had also visited all important places of pilgrimage of all religions, including Lakshmi Narayan temple, has been made here by a soldier of the Indian National Army recently released from confinement, when he interviewed Pandit Prem Parkash Daveshar in Durgiana temple.—F.O.O.C.

[Civil & Military Gazette (Lahore), December 14, 1945]

P. C. Kar, an official in the Governor's House in Bengal when R. G. Casey was the Governor, claimed that the monitoring service at the Governor's House picked up three broadcasts of Netaji on the 31 metre band in December 1945 and January and February 1946.

"... In his first broadcast over Radio Manchuria on 19th December 1945, then under Russian occupation, Netaji stated: " **...We are sure to be successful within two years. I shall go to India on the crest of a third world war and sit in judgment upon those who are trying my officers in the Red Fort.**"

MORE ON RECORD ABOUT NETAJI

(IN RUSSIA)

On August 18, 1945 Netaji was supposed to have died in an air-crash at Taihuku. Yet three months later there were three broadcasts from radio Manchuria, recorded by P.C. Kar, Radio Monitor to the then Governor of West Bengal, which were purported to have been made personally by Subhas Chandra Bose.

In his first broadcast over Radio Manchuria on 19th December 1945, then under Russian occupation, Netaji stated :"We are under the shelter of one of the great powers of the world. We should not be disappointed. The first round of the battle is failure. The battle of freedom is not easy. America won her freedom after 7 years of fighting. Ireland won her freedom after 5 years of fighting. We are sure to be successful within two years. I shall go to India on the crest of a third world war and sit in judgment upon those who are trying my officers in the Red Fort."

[Declassified PMO FILE 870/11/P/16/92 POL]

3. NETAJI'S MESSAGE:FEBRUARY, 1946

"THIS IS SUBHAS CHANDRA BOSE SPEAKING, JAI HIND. IT IS FOR THE THIRD TIME I AM ADDRESSING MY INDIAN BROTHERS AND SISTERS AFTER JAPAN'S SURRENDER.

THE PRIME MINISTER OF ENGLAND IS GOING SEND MR. PETHICK LAWRENCE AND TWO OTHER MINISTERS FROM LONDON WITH NO OBJECT IN VIEW OTHER THAN LET THE BRITISH IMPERIALISM A PERMANENT SETTLEMENT FOR ALL MEANS TO SUCK THE TOTAL BLOOD OF INDIA. NOW, AMONG THESE THREE LONDONERS, ONE HAD TO GO BACK FROM INDIA WITH A BAFFLED HEART ONLY A FEW YEARS AGO.

IT IS AS A SORT OF PRECAUTION, I AM ADVISING INDIANS NOT TO PAY ANY HEED TO THESE IMPOSTERS. I AM SURE THAT MR. PETHICK LAWRENCE WILL HAVE TO SUBMIT AN ADEQUATE EXPLANATION FOR ALL THE MISHAPS AND DISASTERS OF INDIA BY THIS TIME. THE UNDERLYING INTENTION OF THIS ENDEVOUR BY THE THREE IS NOTHING

BUT TO SET A NEW TRAP OF DEPENDENCE IN WHICH INDIA MAY FALL VERY SOON. SO MY EARNEST APPEAL TO THE INDIANS IS THAT THEY SHOULD IN NO CASE HEAR THEM BUT CONTINUE REVOLUTION AGAINST WHAT IS CONTRARY TO ACHIEVE FREEDOM. I THINK MANY OTHER VICEROYS AND MINISTERS WILL EMBARK ON INDIA WITH THE SAME MOTTO FOR KEEPING US IN THE DARK DAWN OF DEPENDENCE. BUT MY INDIANS SHOULD NEVER HEAR THEM."

AGAIN I AM ANNOUNCING THAT WITHIN A SHORT PERIOD OF TWO YEARS INDIA WILL HAVE THE DAWN OF INDEPENDENCE. **WE WILL HAVE COMPLETE FREEDOM BY THAT TIME ANDI WILL ALSO COME BACK IN THE YEAR 1947.**

MANY OF THE INDIANS HAVE DECLARED ME AS THE 'NETAJI' OF INDIA BUT I AM TELLING THEM THAT I AM NOTHING BUT AN HUMBLE SON LIKE OTHERS OF 'BHARAT MATA' AND AM NOT ALL WORTHY OF BEING THE SAME.

THE BRITISH IMPERIALISM WILL HAVE ITS UTTER DESTRUCTION AND IT IS NOW COMMENCED. YOU SEE THEY HAVE COME DOWN TO UTTER SHAME BY KILLING OUR CHILDREN ONLY FOR HAVING THEIR IMPERILISM STILL ABOVE."

Scotland Yard Searching For Netaji

The Strait Times, June 18, 1946, reported: It was reported from London that The Exchange Telegraph in a dispatch from Calcutta said, the newspaper Hindustan Standard had reported that **Scotland Yard and Indian Police authorities were maintaining a vigilant watch along the entire India-Burma border in an effort to capture Subhas Chandra Bose who had been reported 'dead'.**

Indian Daily Mail, 18 June 1946, added: "The newspaper said **travellers crossing the border are being subjected to a careful check and asked if they have seen a bearded Indian Rajah dressed** as a fakir. Intelligence agents are said to believe that if Bose is still alive he has not succeeding in returning to India."

The Chicago Tribune, June 19, 1946 reported: "All over India today it is rumored by the Indian press that Sarat Bose's brother **Subhas Chandra Bose,** former leader... **is trying to cross the Indian border near Tibet in the garb of an Indian fakir. Subhas Bose, easily the Indian most feared by British authorities, if he should return, would throw India into turmoil.** The British assert **he has turned pro-Russian during his exile** thou his brother denied it..."

On July 22, 1946, Khurshed Naoroji, one of Mahatma Gandhi's Secretaries, replying to a letter from Louis Fischer to Gandhiji: remarked: "... There have been many cases of court martial in the Indian army on individuals & platoons during the last war both in India and abroad. There have been mass desertions in the regular army & minor reaps in the N.W.F. Province at the beginning of the last war.

```
the Congress & will have to deal with  them now.    They are going
underground  &  if before the time the Allies (excluding Russia),
have  a  scrap  with Soviet Russia. India is    not satisfied with
the  results  of  the  Constituent  Assembly.  She  will   go over
entirely & absolutely  to  the  enemies of the Allies. The Indian
army  (not  the  Indian  National Army) is no longer of the  same
temper as it was in the first World War. Besides the disaffection
amongst   the   Indian   officers    and   the  rank  &  file,   a
revolutionary   group  has  been working amongst them  & they are
pro-Russian.  There have been many cases of court martial  in the
Indian army on individuals & platoons during the last war both in
India & abroad. There have been  mass desertions  in the  regular
army & minor reaps in the N.W.F.Province at the beginning of  the
last war.

At heart the Indian army is sympathetic with  the Indian National
Army. If Bose comes with the help of Russia neither  Gandhiji nor
the  Congress  will  be  able to reason  with the  country. Also
Russia for propaganda purposes declares itself an Asiatic country
then  there  is  no  hope of any European alliance  acceptable to
India.  Freedom for India under the aegis of Soviet Russia is  no
freedom  for  us;  but it  now rests with England to play fair by
the  people of India or be declared  by us for ever  as the enemy
of India & of the Asiatics. There are other groups in  north India
pro-Russian  ,  but after  Russia joined  the  Allies they lost
caster.  However,  the bitterness towards the English is so great
that  Russia will  again  come  into favour on the  event of any
disagreement amongst the Allies.

Gandhiji  is  not touched with the international reactions but we
can't  afford  to neglect the signs of the time specially when it
concerns our freedom.
```

At heart, the Indian Army is sympathetic with the Indian National Army. **If Bose comes with the help of Russia neither Gandhiji nor the Congress will be able to reason with the country**. Also Russia for propaganda purposes declares itself an Asiatic country then there is no hope of any European alliance acceptable to India..." [Declassified PMO File: 870/11/P/16/92 POL]

It is intriguing that almost a year after the reported air crash at Taihoku, Gandhiji's camp apprehended Netaji's return to India from the Soviet Union instead of being convinced of his death. The correspondent said, there was a possibility that the announcement may coincide with the meeting of the Executive Committee of the All India Forward Bloc in New Delhi on Sept. 14.

"Netaji Arrives In Peshawar"!

On the evening of September 20, Lahore was gripped by an unprecedented sensation when Bradlaugh Hall, Lahore headquarters of the I.N.A., and Sardar Sardul Singh Caveeshar, President of the Forward Bloc, both received identical telegrams emanating from Rawalpindi and reading:-

The telegram was signed "Atam Bodh", the name being that of a Forward Bloc worker of the Frontier Province. The news spread like wildfire throughout the city and newspaper offices were flooded with enthusiastic enquiries.

A telegram call by the Associated Press of India to Dr. Khan Sahib, the premier of the Frontier Province, however ever debunked the whole story as Dr Khan Sahib said he knew nothing about such a happening and if it was true he should have known about it. Dr. Khan Sahib doubted the authenticity of the telegram.

Sardar Sardul Singh Caveeshar told the Associated Press of India, "I do not believe the report is correct, although the telegram is here before us. The telegram may be a bogus one. Atam Bodh is a reliable worker, but some may have played a hoax."

"Netaji Arrives In Peshawar"!

MYSTERIOUS TELEGRAMS

Frontier Gandhi Doubts Authenticity Of Report

LAHORE, Sept. 20.

Lahore was gripped by an unprecedented sensation this evening when Bradlaugh Hall, Lahore headquarters of the I.N.A., and Sardar Sardul Singh Caveeshar, President of the Forward Bloc, both received identical telegrams emanating from Rawalpindi and reading:—

"Netaji arrived Peshawar"

The telegram was signed "Atam Bodh", the name being that of a Forward Bloc worker of the Frontier Province.

The news spread like wild fire throughout the city and newspaper offices were flooded with enthusiastic enquiries.

A telephone call by the Associated Press of India to Dr. Khan Sahib, the Premier of the Frontier Province, however debunked the whole story as Dr. Khan Sahib said he knew nothing about such a happening, and if it was true he should have known about it.

Dr. Khan Sahib doubted the autenticity of the telegram.

Sardar Sardul Singh Caveeshar told the Associated Press of India, "I do not believe the report is correct, although the telegram is here before us. The telegram may be a bogus one. Atam Bodh is a reliable worker, but some may have played a hoax".—(A.P.)

...ace, for libel unless he retracted a statement, which, Pearson said, indicated that he "filched" from Commerce Department the files of Mr. Wallace's Russian letter to President Truman.

It was because, it was understood, that Pearson would publish the letter to-day that Mr Charles Ross, Presidential Secretary, last night disclosed its text without first consulting President Truman.

"This document came into my possession in an open and above board fashion from sources which had no connection with the Department, Mr. Pearson stated.—Reuter

ORISSA PREMIER MEETS VICEROY

NEW DELHI, Sept. 20.

Mr. Hare Krishna Mahtab, Premier of Orissa had an interview with the Viceroy to-day.—(A.P.)

[Amrita Bazar Patrika: 21 September 1946]

The Bose mystery was heightened by a report in the Nationalist circles in Peshawar. It was reported on September 20, 1946, that **"Bose, it was claimed, entered the U.S.S.R. via China. After spending some time in Russia, he went to Afghanistan. About two months before he returned to India, stayed here for a few days and then resumed his onward journey between Kabul and Peshawar. It was added, was performed under the cover of a veil that Bose was wearing on his arrival in Peshawar."**

In September 1946, the next and most sensational news appeared that Netaji was in Frontier as a guest of Fakir of Ipi.

Netaji In Frontier:

Guest Of Fakir Of Ipi

It was reported on 23 September 1946: "The Sind Forward Bloc weekly "Tomorrow" states that **Netaji was the guest of Fakir of Ipi and was hale and hearty despite the recent bombing operations.**

Quoting a letter dated September 9, stated to be in Netaji's own handwriting, as its authority for the information, the paper says,"**Netaji was in South East Asia till April this year and was twice spotted by the British Intelligence but with the help of some European powers he managed to reach Europe from where he arrived in the Frontier where the Fakir of Ipi placed all his resources at Netaji's disposal.**"

Amrita Bazar Patrika dated 26 September 1946 published the same report: "**Subhas Chandra Bose is a respectable guest of the Fakir of Ipi and he is hale and hearty in spite of the indiscriminate bombing by the Royal Indian Air Force,**according to the "Morrow", a weekly Forward Bloc organ.

The paper also quoted a letter dated Sept. 9 in Netaji's own handwriting as its authority for information and adds that **Netaji was in South-East Asia command up to April this year.**

According to this paper, **Netaji was spotted twice in South-East Asia by army intelligence circles but with the help of some foreign powers, he managed to visit Europe from where he arrived at the frontier of India, where he is now a guest of the Fakir of Ipi.**The paper adds that the Fakir has placed all his resources and men at his disposal.

The paper alleges that **the motive behind the recent bombing of Waziristan was apparently to kill Netaji.**"

Frontier News dated 29 September 1946 from Peshawar was that Khan Abad Khan, President of the N.W.F.P. Forward Bloc was emphatic that "**Subhas Chandra Bose is alive and would shortly join them**".

NETAJI HALE AND HEARTY

Living As Guest Of Fakir Of Ipi

Mr. Subhas Chandra Bose is a respectable guest of the Fakir of Ipi and is hale and hearty in spite of the indiscriminate bombing by the Royal Indian Air Force, according to the "Morrow", a weekly Forward Bloc organ.

The paper quotes a letter dated Sept. 9 in Netaji's own handwriting as its authority for information and adds that Netaji was in South-East Asia command up to April this year.

According to this paper Netaji was spotted twice in South-East Asia by army intelligence circles, but with the help of some foreign powers he managed to visit Europe from where he arrived at the frontier of India, where he is now a guest of the Fakir of Ipi.

The paper adds that the Fakir has placed all his resources and men at his disposal.

The paper alleges that the motive behind the recent bombing of Waziristan was apparently to kill Netaji.

[Amrita Bazar Patrika: 26 September 1946]

The Windsor Star reported on October 19, 1946: **Bose Plans to "Return".**Free Indian leader was believed dead. **Subhas Chandra**

Bose leader of the "Free Indian Government" supported by the Japanese in 1942, plans to **"return from the dead"** later this month, Indian sources claimed Friday.

"... Indian informants said they learned of the Bose plan from members of the Indian military mission in Germany. They saidthe story was supported also by members of the former Indian National Army. The former military men reportedly said that **Bose "definitely" wasstill aliveand that his reappearance was scheduled for October 21, the anniversary of the formation of the Azad Hind (free government).**

"Bose was reported either en route from Turkey or the guest of the Fakir of Ipi heads Waziristan tribal activities against the British. ...Pandit Jawaharlal Nehru's visit to the northwestern frontier was believed possibly connected with the Bose plan."

"Some reports declare that Congressmen believe that Gandhi's inner voice is secret information which he has received. It is possible to think that they were boosting Russia rather than being serious about Bose; of all the rumours those due to Congress merit the greatest attention. This means that Gandhi holds the answer.

We have nothing in the way of intelligence which helps directly to disclose the grounds Gandhi has for saying what he did or the reasons why he did so. There is however a secret report which says that **Nerhru received a letter from Bose saying he was in Russia and that he wanted to escape to India. He would come via Chitral where one of Sarat Bose's sons should meet him. The information alleges that Gandhi and Sarat Bose are among those who are aware of this.** The story is unlikely but the points has to be noted that if the story has any foundation in fact, it is probable that the letter from Bose arrived about the time Gandhi made his public statement. In January also Sarat Bose is reported to have said that he was convinced his brother was alive.

The information received from internal sources is puzzling and the same can be said about external information. On the 7th of January, the Russian paper *Pravda* denied in strong terms that Bose was in Russia. Before then, however, the Ghilzai Malang ..."

Civil & Military Gazette (Lahore), dated 9th January 1946 reported from London that according to the Moscow radio, the Soviet journalist, David Zaslvsky wrote an article in "Pravada".

"Zaslvsky referred to a report, which, he said, appeared in some Indian newspapers on December 31, and declared: "The language of unscrupulous liars begins to penetrate also the political jungle of India."

"... The substance of the fairy tale is as follows: ... Subhas Chandra Bose, ...has allegedly fled to Russia and has allegedly been there since the unconditional surrender of Japan, together with his soldiers of the 'Indian National Army', who were taken prisoner by the Russian Army."

"... alleged to have freely traveled in Soviet countries and inspected his. 300,000-strong army. "But the story does not end here. An unnamed soldier appears to know that responsible representatives of the Soviet Government conferred with Bose and gave this... adventurer imaginary, concrete promises."

In December of the year of grace 1946, a report circulating in the higher echilions of diplomatic circles makes mention of the fact that the then Governor of the province of Khost in Afghanistan had been informed by the Russian Ambassador in Kabul that, **"there were Congress refugees in Moscow and Bose was included in their numbers."**

"NEWS FROM TEHERAN"

2.   Another report received from Teheran stated that the Russian Vice-Consul General Moradoff disclosed that, "Bose was in Russia, where he was organising a group of Russians to work on the same line as the INA for the complete Freedom of India". This report mentions that it was sometimes in March, 1946 that Moradoff made this disclosure.

[Declassified PMO Political File No. 800/6/C/3/88 -Pol]

Another report received from Teheran stated that the Russian Vice-Consul General Maoradoff disclosed that, **"Bose was in Russia, where he was organising a group of Russians to work on the same line as the INA for the complete Freedom of India"**. This report mentions that it was sometime in March 1946 that Moradoff made this disclosure.

Some reports declare that Congressmen believe that Gandhis inner voice is secret information which he as received. Communists are concerned in only one of th remours reported. It is possible to think that they were boosting Russia rather than being serious about Bose: xi of all the rumours those due to Congress mrit the greatest attention. This means that Gandhi holds the answer.

We have nothing in the way of intelligence which helps directly to disclose the grounds Gandhi has for saying what he did or the reasons why he did so. There is, however, a secret report which says that Nehru received a letter from Bose hxx saying he was in Russia and that he wanted to escape to India. He would come via Chitral where one of Srat Bose's sons should meet him. The information alleges that Gandhi and Sarat Bose are among those who are aware of this. The story is unlikely but the points has to be noted that if the story has any foundation in fact, it is probable that the letter from Bose arrived about the time Gandhi made his public statement. In January also Sarat Bose is reported to have said that he was convinced his brother was alive.

Another piece of intelligence which connects Bose with the N.W.Frontier is a letter written by the President of the Frontie Students Congress. In this letter the writer said that Bose was in T.T. and that the writer was going there himself. The date of the letter was not stated in the report received.

[Declassified File No. 273/INA/C-4/Part IV; Page: 38]

The British Intelligence Bureau reveals the most intriguing information connecting Netaji Subhas Chandra Bose with the

North-West Frontier [Declassified File No. 273/INA/Part IV; Page: 38]: "**Another piece of intelligence that connects Bose with the N.W. Frontier is a letter written by the President of the Frontier Students Congress. In this letter, the writer said that Bose was on T.T. and that the writer was going there himself.**The date of the letter was not stated in the report received."

"NEWS FROM RUSSIAN AMBASSADOR TO AFGHANISTAN"

1.   In december of the year of grace 1946 a report circulating in the higher echilons of diplomatic circles makes mention of the fact that the then Governor of the province of Khost in Afghanistan had been informed by the Russian Ambassador in Kabul that, "there were Congress refugees in Moscow and Bose was included in their numbers."

[Declassified PMO Political File No. 800/6/C/3/88 -Pol]

CHAPTER SEVEN

Pandit Nehru's 'Mission Of Love'

On 14 September 1946, it was reported that Pandit Nehru as head of the new Interim India Government had directed British Imperial troops for the stoppage of air and artillery bombardment of recalcitrant tribesmen in South Waziristan on the North West frontier.

An official announcement on the subject was expected in a day or two when confirmation of the execution of these orders had been received from the local authorities.

Following the stoppage of recent bombing operations in Waziristan, it was gathered that the whole question of Frontier policy was proposed and considered in order to evolve more satisfactory methods of dealing with tribesmen. In this task, it was hoped to enlist the cooperation of tribesmen themselves.

The need for a new policy was believed to have been brought to the forefront as the result of a review made by Pandit Nehru and his colleagues of the situation created by the Waziristan bombing. The operations there began on August 1 against the Shabi Khels who were a small part of the Mahsuds. Some villages were reported to have been destroyed. But casualties had not exceeded four or five. When these facts came to light early in September, inquiries were made with a view to putting an end to the operations in a satisfactory way. The bombing had now stopped it was expected that the whole matter would be satisfactorily settled.

Nehru intended to visit Frontier tribal areas in the middle of October. It was reported that contrary to the League propaganda, Faqir of Ipi made a statement supporting the formation of the Interim Government and hoping it would bring relief to the tribal people.

Five thousand green-uniformed Muslim League volunteers carrying lances, spears and staves, demonstrated at Peshawar Aerodrome as Pandit Nehru arrived to begin a tour of the North-West Frontier area of India. The volunteers shouted: "Nehru go back. Down with the unholy alliance between the British and the Hindus. British and Indian troops with bayonets fixed were posted inside and outside the aerodrome. Armed military and police pickets stood ready at strategic points on the route from the airfield to the residence of Dr Khan Sahib, Congress Prime Minister of the North-West Frontier Province.

"I am deeply interested in the welfare of tribal territory," said Nehru replying to greetings sent by tribal chieftains. He added: "We want to approach them as friends and try to understand their difficulties and remove them.

It is not our desire to interfere with the freedom they possess, but rather to help them in every way to better their condition. We should like them to come into closer contact with their neighbours in the Frontier Province, and in India as a whole, so that we may get to know each other better."

But tribesmen opened fire as Nehru visited the Frontier outpost. Artillery returned their fire. Firing continued in a desultory fashion throughout the day. The tribesmen were adherents of the Faqir of Ipi, the red-bearded chieftain, who for 20 years had led a movement for tribal independence in North Waziristan.

The vengeful tribesmen, crouching behind rocks and shrubs in the sun-scorched North-West Frontier hills, opened fire on the Razmak outpost township as the aircraft bringing Jawaharlal Nehru, Vice-President of the Interim Government, and his party arrived. British artillery in the town returned the fire, which continued desultorily throughout the day. The tribesmen, in the sniping technique, used at least a 20-millimeter cannon, stripped from a crashed British aircraft, and a 3.7 mountain gun, as well as rifles.

The marksmen were reported to be the adherents of the Faqir of Ipi, who was said to have a cave hideout in the gaunt Waziristan hills near the Afghan border, about 20 miles from Razmak, Waziristan. Nehru had met two Jigras (representative assemblies) of the tribesmen and had been coldly received in each case. At a North Waziristan frontier township, Mirahsah Maliks (leaders) walked out of a Jigra that had been specially arranged for Pandit Nehru.

In Razmak town the second Jigra was also hostile. The tribesmen told Nehru that they did not consider him as their leader, but that they considered their leader to be Jinnah, President of the Muslim League.

Pandit Nehru accompanied by Abdul Ghaffar Khan and Khan Sahib, Frontier Premier, went into the heart of tribal territory which had all those years been a land of mystery to Indians. Before leaving Peshawar by air for Miranshah in North Waziristan, community Ghaffar Khan, at a Press conference, explainedthatit was a fact-finding and goodwill mission of Nehru.

The tribesmen, who were the kith and kin of the Frontier people, both by religion and culture, should be won over by love and not by force: they must have a new deal. "I have faith in non-violence,"

Khan declared, "and I would apply that principle to the solution of that among the Frontier problem."

WAZIRISTAN TRIBESMEN

Nehru Orders Stoppage Of Air & Artillery Bombardment

NEW DELHI, Sept. 13.

It is reliably learnt that Pandit Jawaharlal Nehru, Member in charge of the External Affairs portfolio in the Interim Government, has already issued orders for the stoppage of air and artillery bombardment of recalcitrant tribesmen in South Waziristan.

An official announcement on the subject is expected in a day or two when confirmation of the execution of these orders has been received from the local authorities.

Following the stoppage of recent bombing operations in Waziristan, it is gathered that the whole question of Frontier policy is proposed to be reconsidered in order to evolve more satisfactory methods of dealing with tribesmen. In this task it is hoped to enlist the co-operation of tribesmen themselves.

The need for a new policy is believed to have been brought to the forefront as the result of a review made by Pandit Nehru and his colleagues of the situation created by the Waziristan bombing. The operations there began on August 1 against the Shabi Khels who are a small part of the Mahsuds. Some villages are reported to have been destroyed. But casualties have not exceeded four or five. When these facts came to light early in September, enquiries were made with a view to putting an end to the operations in a satisfactory way. Latest reports show that bombing has now stopped and very soon the whole matter will be satisfactorily settled.—(A.P.)

NO-CONFIDEN
BENGAL

Motions To
On Sept. 1

CONGRESS PAI
PART IN BUD

Two no-confidence motions,
and the other against the Chief

[Amrita Bazar Patrika: 15 September 1946]

Khan stated that the hostile demonstrations in Peshawar were engineered by the Political Department which had tried their best to prevent Nehruji from visiting Waziristan, "Besides Political Department officers, there are others whom I do not wish to name who too did not like Nehruji visiting the heart of the tribal country. Since Nehraji had the audacity to disobey their wishes, they planned to teach him a lesson.

Making his first public reference in the course of his tour to tribal policy, Pt. Nehru said in a speech in South Waziristan on October 19 that a correct approach to the inhabitants of the tribal areas was one of love and faith on both sides. Although huge sums had been spent in the past, the old policy had proved a failure.

"You cannot win over a people by punitive expeditions," said Pandit Nehru adding: "You can only win them over by love. Crime must be eradicated. But even here according to the most modern principles, the causes of 'crime' should be deeper, calling for radical curative methods such as education and an alteration of the economic environment. To this end, we must bend our efforts."

It was reported from Landikotal (Khyber Pass) that several hundred tribesmen attacked Pandit Jawaharlal Nehru's convoy the next day within a quarter of a mile of the gate of Landi-Kotal Fort, resulting in a sharp brief battle between Khyber riflemen and tribesmen. Between 300 and 400 shots were fired.

"Only minor injuries were reported as a result of the clash which was one of three during the trip from Peshawar to the Afghan frontier and return.

Landikotal is 34 miles along the Khyber Pass Road from Peshawar and is only about five miles on the Afghan frontier. The attack occurred on a twisting section of the road which is flanked on both sides by towering cliffs." the report said.

Pandit Nehru refused to change his plans after a five-minute gun battle between hostile tribesmen and his military escort in the

Khyber Pass. He was involved in an exchange of shots between the military escort and several hundred tribesmen within a quarter of a mile of the gate of Andikotal Fort. He continued his journey to Peshawar with a reinforced escort.

Meetings of tribesmen were being held and arranged everywhere to be addressed by Nehruji. It was in the air that "Netaji Is Alive" and Panditji had wish for friendship with Faqir of Ipi.

The Faqir of Ipi, the sworn enemy of the Interim Government, "respite of the British, who was recently reported to have given asylum to Netaji, welcoming Nehruji,said: "I will call my jirga and am ready to meet him if he wants to meet me but as long as the British are paper trusts eagles ... how can I go to ... meet him?"

On 21 October 1946, Pandit Nehru was injured by glass splinters when the car in which he was travelling was stoned after leaving Malakand for Peshawar. Abdul Gaffar Khan, leader of Congress Muslims on the North West Frontier, and Dr. Khan Sahib Khan, chief minister of the North West Frontier Provincial Government, who were travelling with Pandit Nehru were also said to have been slightly injured. Pandit Nehru was returning to Peshawar on the last full day of his tour of the North West Frontier area. He is due to leave for New Delhi by air tomorrow.

Frontier Minister Mehrechand Khanna alleged that the Political Department was working hand in glove with the League. "Otherwise how did Leaguers know of Pandit Nehru's programme when it was supposed to be secret and even the Frontier Ministry did not know it?" he asked.

Meetings of tribesmen were being arranged everywhere to be addressed by Pandit Nehru, to meet the tribesmen individually to discuss their problems and convey a message of goodwill on behalf of the Interim Government and the Indian people.

Rumours of the discovery of a plot by Muslim fanatics to assassinate Nehru during his visit were circulating in Peshawar.

Later, in the Central Legislative Assembly, Pandit Nehru said, there was a great deal of violence during his visit to the North-West Frontier Province and tribal areas. Various opinions could be formed and inferences were drawn as to who was behind this "organised violence".

However, according to a report by 'The Windsor Star' dated October 19, 1946, the purpose of Pandit Nehru's visit to the North-West Frontier Province was possibly different.

It reported: **'Bose was reported either en route from Turkey or the guest of the Fakir of Ipi heads Waziristan tribal activities against the British. ...Pandit Jawaharlal Nehru's visit to the north-western frontier was believed possiblyconnected with the Bose plan.'**

On 1st November, in response to a question at the Centre's meeting, Pandit Nehru said that border expansion and border revision would be done to enter the North West Sea. Aryan conflict had been going on for a long time. An invitation book or limit was currently being followed on this answer policy. It was now being considered with leaf caution and instruments.

In response to the apocalypse of the other party, Nehru said that the government had no desire to have a dispute with anyone. It would be happy if friendly relations could be established with Faqir of Ipi.

He said that he had received many compliments. Some of them were from poets who claimed to be friends of Faqir of Ipi, and some were written by Faqir himself. But deciphering the signature names was difficult. It was said in three readings that he wanted to come into contact with Pandit Nehru. Nehru said that he did not give any reply to the fake letters that he received, but he would be happy if he could get in touch with and reestablish the matter with him.

Bose Coming "Forward"

SUBHAS BOSE
"Still Plans Free India"

Burdwan (Bengal), Friday.—Subhas Chandra Bose, Indian Nationalist leader, reported by Tokio last August to have been killed in an air crash, is not only alive, but "prosecuting a plan to make India free," according to Mr. H. V. Kamath, former member of the Indian Civil Service, who resigned to become a leader of Bose's extreme Left "forward bloc" party.

To-day he observed that "the British Empire is now between two ghosts—the ghost of Hitler in Europe, and the supposed ghost of Bose in Asia.", All members of the "forward bloc" (at present an illegal body) had decided to join the National Congress party, he said.—Reuter

[Liverpool Daily Post: 22 December 1945]

On 22 December 1945, the Liverpool Daily Post reported a piece of sensational news: 'Subhas Chandra Bose, Indian Nationalist leader, reported by Tokyo last August to have been killed in an air crash, is not only alive but **"prosecuting a plan to make India free**," according to Mr. H.V Kamath, a former member of the Indian Civil Service, who resigned to become a leader of Bose's extreme left "Forward Bloc" party.

Today he observed that "the British Empire is now between two ghosts -the ghost of Hitler in Europe, and the supposed ghost of Bose in Asia." All members of the "Forward Bloc" (at present an illegal body) had decided to join the National Congress party, he said.'

On August 22, 1946, the Amrita Bazar Patrika dropped a bombshell. It reported from its Allahabad Office:

Subhas Bose To Come Out On October 21?

The hope is being expressed in local Forward Bloc circles that **Mr. Subhas Chandra Bose will appear in public on October 21** the day scheduled to be observed in commemoration of the Azad Hind Government all over the country. The Secretary of All India Forward Bloc in the course of a circular letter to all presidents and general secretaries of the Provincial Forward Blocs also appealed to the Congress and the nation to wholeheartedly make the celebrations a grand success.

On September 6, 1946, the Amrita Bazar Patrika reported another sensational news on Netaji being alive:

"Netaji Is Alive"

Hope Of Re-Appearance In Indian Scene Soon

Subhas Bose To Come Out On October 21?

ALLAHABAD, Aug. 19.

The hope is being expressed in local Forward Bloc circles that Mr. Subhas Chandra Bose will appear in public on October 21 the day scheduled to be observed in commemoration of the Azad Hind Government all over the country. The Secretary, All-India Forward Bloc in course of a circular letter to all presidents and general secretaries of the Provincial Forward Blocs also appealed to the Congress and the nation to wholeheartedly make the celebrations a grand success.—(U.P.)

[Amrita Bazar Patrika: 22 August 1946]

"Subhas Chandra Bose is alive and quite hale and hearty" This statement was made by Mr Bishambar Dayal Tripathi, M.L.A. (U.P.), General Secretary of the Forward Bloc, according to our Jhansi correspondent. The correspondent says: "Mr Tripathi who was on his way from Jubbulpore to Lucknow broke the journey at Jhanshi for a few hours. He stated that Netaji Subhas Chandra Bose is definitely alive and quite hale and hearty and will be amongst us very soon.

"When pressed to give an approximate date of Netaji's re-appearance on the Indian scene" the correspondent adds" Tripathi stated that a very important and sensational announcement regarding Netaji Bose and his whereabouts will be made by Sept. 20 or by the end of this month at the latest. Mr. Tripathi did not mention any specific date for this announcement."

It was reported that Pandit Yajee, Vice-President of Forward Bloc had given notice of a resolution for the next AICC meeting urging the election of Netaji as the next Congress President and that Pandit Nehru should broadcast an appeal to Netaji to come to India immediately.

"Netaji Is Alive"

Hope Of Re-Appearance In Indian Scene Soon

(From Our Allahabad Office.)

WEDNESDAY, Sept. 4.

"Subhas Chandra Bose is alive and quite hale and hearty" this statement was made by Mr. Bishambar Dayal Tripathi, M.L.A. (U. P.), General Secretary of the All-India Forward Bloc, according to our Jhansi correspondent.

The correspondent says: "Mr. Tripathi who was on his way from Jubbulpore to Lucknow broke journey at Jhansi for a few hours. He stated that Netaji Subhas Chandra Bose is definitely alive and quite hale and hearty and will be amongst us soon—very soon.

"When pressed to give an approximate date of Netaji's re-appearance on the Indian scene" the correspondent adds" Mr. Tripathi stated that a very important and sensational announcement regarding Netaji Bose and his whereabouts will be made by Sept. 20 or by the end of this month at the latest. Mr. Tripathi did not mention any specific date for this announcement."

The correspondent says, there is a possibility that the announcement may coincide with the meeting of the Executive Committee of the All-India Forward Bloc at New Delhi on Sept. 14.

[Amrita Bazar Patrika: 6 September 1946]

Subhas Bose Is Alive

Forward Bloc Working Committee's Assertion

NEW DELHI, Sept. 16.

The Working Committee of the All-India Forward Bloc asserted to-day that Mr. Subhas Chandra Bose is alive and will reappear at the opportune time "for the final revolution in order to free India from foreign yoke".

The Committee, which met under the presidentship of Sardar Sardul Singh Caveesher, said in a resolution, "for sometime reports have been frequently appearing in the Press to the effect that Netaji Subhas Chandra Bose s n India and will reappear soon in our midst. In the opinion of the Committee such news has no basis in fact but the Committee is in a position to declare that Netaji is still alive and will reappear at the opportune time for the final revolution in order to free India from foreign yoke. The Committee calls upon Forward Bloc units to prepare the country for the final stage of revolution to be led by Subhas Chandra Bose".—(A. P.)

[Amrita Bazar Patrika: 17 September 1946]

Netaji To Reappear This Month

The unqualified assertion that "**Netaji Subhas Chandra Bose is going to make his appearance on a certain date and at a certain place within a short time**" was made by Prof. Mota Singh, President of the Punjab Forward Bloc and a close associate of the I.N.A. leader at Lahore on September 9. 1946.

The seventy year old Professor who was addressing a meeting of Forward Bloc workers at the residence of Sardar Sardul Singh Caveeshar, Chairman of the All India Forward Bloc, asked by the Associated Press of India to elaborate his statement said: I am not prepared at present to go into further details regarding Bose's reappearance. My information is based on a reliable source through the agency of the I.N.A.

On September 8, Professor Mota Singh speaking at a meeting made the same prediction when he said that **Subhas Bose was expected to discover himself before the end of that month.** He appealed to his audience to maintain an atmosphere of cordiality and communal harmony which above everything else were the creed of Subhas Chandra Bose.

The Working Committee of the All India Forward Bloc asserted on September 16, that **Subhas Chandra Bose was alive and would reappear at the opportune time for the final revolution in order to free India from foreign yoke.**

The Committee, which met under the presidentship of Sardar Sardul Singh Caveesher, said in a resolution, "for some time reports have been frequently appearing in the Press to the effect that Netaji Subhas Chandra Bose is in India and will reappear soon in our midst. In the opinion of the Committee, such news has no basis but the Committee is in a position to declare that Netaji is still alive and will reappear at the opportune time for the final revolution in order to free India from foreign yoke. The Committee calls upon Forward Bloc units to prepare the country for the final stage of the revolution to be led by Subhas Chandra Bose.

The Working Committee of the All India Forward Bloc urged the central and provincial governments not to use foreign troops to quell civil strife and to depend instead on the strength of their own people. **The committee demanded the immediate release of all political labour and I.N.A. personnel whether convicted of violence or otherwise and condemned the bombing of Frontier tribesmen.**

On September 29, 1946, the Civil & Military Gazette (Lahore) reported that **Khan Abad Khan, President of the North-West Frontier Province Forward Bloc was emphatic that "Subhas Chandra Bose is alive" and would shortly join them.**

Sheel Bhadra Yajee, Vice President of the All India Forward Bloc from Patna, expressed surprise at Pandit Nehru's statement confirming Netaji's death and said: I must ask the public to remember recently a respectable body like the Working Committee of the Forward Bloc passed a resolution to the effect that Netaji is alive and would appear in India at the opportune moment.

"I can only say this authoritative Statement was based on reliable material. I would not like to say anything more at present except reassuring the masses that liberator Netaji is still in flesh and blood."

On 19 October 1946, it was reported that the Indian Daily Mail's leader criticising Pandit Nehru's statement on Netaji's death as hasty and ill-advised received wide publicity in the Indian Press. Similar views were expressed by Mr. Saojee, a prominent Congressman from the Central Provinces, who said: "Pandit Nehru's statement contains nothing new. Subhas Chandra Bose is alive but not in India. "Arrangements are being made to bring him into India by his trusted Forward Bloc colleagues all there is strong ground to hope that Netaji will be back soon."

On October 22, Aurobindo Bose, Netaji's nephew, declared in Karachi that Netaji was alive and would reappear at an opportune moment. He, however, refused to divulge Netaji's present whereabouts. According to Forward Bloc leaders, Netaji was expected to reappear on October 24.

It was reported three days later that addressing a vast meeting in Lahore, Sardar Sardul Singh Caveeshar, the Forward Bloc President asserted that Netaji is still alive. "I have conclusive proof Netaji is alive and I have come across businessmen who saw Netaji in Singapore after the plane crash in which he was reported killed ngase's trusted Secret Service men of INA, Dr. Pabitra Mohan Roy and Haridas Mitra were among the four prioners still convicted under the Enemy Agents Ordinance. It was at that time when the Home Department, Government of India issued a communication to the INA Enquiry and Relief Committee that the cases of those prisoners had been referred to the Government of Bengal. The cases of Col. Burhanuddin, Captain Rashid, Captain Singara Singh, Captain Fateh Khan, and other INA prisoners had been forwarded to the Defence Department.

Mrs. Leela Roy, one of the most trusted followers of Bose, Forward Bloc leader and member of the Constituent Assembly, and Mr Anil Roy left for Noakhali by air to visit the riot-affected areas in East Bengal. A batch of volunteers, including six lady workers of the National Service Institute accompanied them. But where was Bose?

Pandit Sheel Bhadra Yajee, vice-president of the All-India Forward Bloc, said in a statement from Patna that he would like to "assure the masses that liberator Netaji Subhas Chandra Bose is still in flesh and blood."

Refuting the statement of Jawaharlal Nehru who had expressed his conviction, based on a letter received by him from Col. Habibur Rahaman, that all rumours suggesting that Subhas Chandra Bose is alive, are without foundation, Yajee said.

"Very recently, the working committee of the **All-India Forward Bloc had passed a resolution that it was in a position to state that Netaji was alive and would reappear in India at the opportune moment.** I can only say at present." declared Yajee, that **this authoritative statement was based on reliable materials.**"

In November 1946, Caveeshar again said at Lahore that the "Singapore announcement definitely establishing Subhas Chandra Bose's death" was a made-up affair" and had no more value than that of Col. Habibur Rahaman."

"**I am positive that Netaji is alive,**" asserted Caveeshar. He said, "**Some of the Forward Bloc members have received code messages from Netaji Subhas Chandra Bose which are as recent as three months ago. That code was known to Netaji and no one else.**"

On January 12, 1947, Caveeshar, in a conference in Arrah, Bihar outlined a ten point programme for achieving independence.
The programme includes **making the armed forces and the Police nationalist minded, training people in the use of firearms, organizing Azad Hind Dals all over the country on the lines of the I.N.A., bringing together all Asiatic countries now suffering under European and American exploitation, and turning the Constituent Assembly into a revolutionary body.** Caveeshar declared that the British offer of freedom was neither sincere nor wholehearted. The people must, therefore, organise and wrest power.

Soon, the revival ceremony of the "Forward Bloc" weekly founded by Netaji was held at Asutosh College Library Hall in Calcutta. Sjta. Leela Roy who would edit the journal, said, it was first published by Netaji on August 5, 1939. Its publication was suspended on October 31, 1940, as this journal was never in the good books of the Government. After a great effort, it was possible to obtain sanction from the Government to publish it again.

Caveeshar paid a warm tribute to Mrs. Leela Roy, a lifelong follower of Netaji, who had been associated with the publication of the journal in the past. He said that the Congress leadership might not make revolutionary use of the Constituent Assembly for which the Forward Bloc would always press.

In May 1947, Caveeshar stressed the **need for an All India organisation of I.N.A. armed and equipped both for internal security and defence purposes and appealed for a Rs. 10 Crore fund for this purpose.** Caveeshar urged the people to be **"prepared to seize power by strengthening our forces by military training as compromises and conferences won't realise the dream of Netaji. Congress seems to be giving up the ideal of undivided India to placate the Muslim League but we must gird our lions and oppose Pakistan at all costs and establish Swaraj for the masses in a classless society for which the Forward Bloc stands."**

Caveeshar at a press conference in Nagpur declared it was the Bloc's firm conviction that the **Peoples Government could only be established by a military coup and so they are organising a military force on the lines of the Azad Hind Fauj.**

Reiterating that India is indivisible, Caveeshar said independence with a price of division is worth nothing. Division could be prevented only by a fight and the Congress was not ready for the fight. The Forward Bloc would have to undertake this task. If India is to be freed, they should come out of the Constituent Assembly which was a mere waste of money, and organise the Azad Hind Fauj in every town and hamlet.

It was learnt that the next session of the Forward Bloc would consider the question of merging the Forward Bloc with the I.N.A. and forging one strong organisation. Many I.N.A. officers would attend the session. Meanwhile, Dr. Lakshmi of the Rani of Jhansi Regiment of the I.N.A. was undertaking a tour of Sind to promote communal harmony.

Mukundalal Sircar, Secretary, of All India Forward Bloc while addressing a public meeting at Habiganj said, "In spite of all the false and mischievous propaganda that is being carried on to distract our mind, I am in a position to declare categorically that Netaji Subhas Chandra Bose is alive and shall make his appearance at the right moment." Sircar and the party were on a tour of Assam and Surma Valley propagating the ideals of revolution as envisaged by Netaji Subhas Chandra Bose. After visiting Silchar, Badarpur, Karimganj, and Habiganj they left for Sylhet and Shillong.

On June 14, 1947, Pandit Sheel Bhadra Yajee, General Secretary of the All India Forward Bloc addressing the Bihar Forward Bloc Executive in Patna declared that **they would resist the division of India at all costs and raise a force of million men which would work on the lines of Azad Hind Fauj.** The meeting resolved reiterating the stand of the Forward Bloc for the establishment of the Union of Socialist Republics of India and rejecting the latest British plan for the transfer of power.

On June 23, Daya Shanker Misra, the General Secretary of the District Forward Bloc, Fatehpur said, "**Netaji Subhas Chandra is definitely alive and will be in India before the end of the year to take a leading part, especially in the U.P., in the final freedom movement of India.**"

Misra declared that **he was put in possession of this "indisputable" information in a letter from Netaji Bose himself, given to him by a colleague of the leader somewhere in the outskirts of Nainital,** to secure which Mr Misra "placed his own life in danger."

It was understood that the Forward Bloc members would shortly resign from the Congress and join hands in the I.N.A. and fight elections in the Legislatures and local bodies on the issue of a United India and Indian Union of Socialist Republics.

On April 28, 1947, stories were reported about the appearance of Netaji Subhas Chandra Bose at Patna and the villages visited by Gandhiji.

The villagers said that after the visit of Gandhiji to a riot-devastated village, a Sanyasi appeared and they had strong reasons to believe that the Sanyasi was no other than Netaji Subhas Chandra Bose.
In some villages visited by Gandhiji, the people had talks with him and he stated that he was not Netaji but asked them to rest assured that Netaji was alive.

At some places, the people tried to take a snap of the Sanyasi but he left the scene on one pretext or another. It was reported that the same Sanyasi was at the Patna junction a day after Gandhiji left Patna for Delhi.'

In March 1946 Gandhiji expressed his belief that '**Bose is alive**' and even in April 1947, he was assuring the riot-devastated villagers that Bose was alive at that time.

At that point, Sarat Chandra Bose planned to fulfill Netaji's cause. In July 1947, he said, "The Domination and exploitation of the two Indias by British Imperialism would continue in a subtle and insidious form in the name of Dominion status. The sufferings and sacrifices of the people in the cause of Indian unity and independence, and the heroic fight put up outside India's borders by Indian civilians and soldiers under Netaji's leadership had not yielded the desired results. Hence the need for a conference."

On July 12, 1947, Leftist and I.N.A. leaders met at a close-door conference convened by Sarat Chandra Bose at Calcutta. A prominent Forward Bloc leader later hinted at the possibility of the formation of a United Leftist Party consisting of Forward Bloc members, I.N.A. men, and others.

[Jugantar: 15 March 1946]

The National Congress had accepted the Mountbatten Plan. On that ground that since the party was no more anti-imperialistic, in August 1947 the All India Forward Bloc Executive Committee decided that no member of the Bloc should be a member of the National Congress and Bloc should henceforth function as a separate party.

CIA had a keen interest in the latest developments in Forward Bloc. One CIA report distributed on 10 September 1948 says: '**In Bengal, the Forward Bloc is divided into seven sections.** The leader of the Forward Bloc is Sri Silbhadra Jajee (Sheel Bhadra Yajee), who wants to consolidate a strong leftist group. Other important members are Sri Hemanta Bose and Sri Bimal Ghose. ...'

On January 28, 1949, Sarat Chandra Bose told a public meeting in Kolkata, that he believed his brother Subhas Chandra Bose was still alive.

On July 24, 1949, R.S. Ruikar, General Secretary of the All India Forward Bloc issued a circular to his party units throughout the country. Netaji Subhas Chandra Bose was presumed by some to be in Communist-occupied China and might come back to India provided that the ban on his entry into the country is withdrawn. Mr Ganguly, President of U.P. Forward Bloc in an informal talk with the UPI at Benares, disclosed this information. The party units were asked to hold public meetings in their respective centers to press the government to adopt necessary action in this regard.

On February 7, 1950, The Civil & Military Gazette (Lahore) reported: "Leaders of the All India Forward Bloc including General Mohan Singh and Comrade Sheel Bhadra Yajee declared that **Subhas Chandra Bose was alive and that the freedom movement started by him would be continued...**"

The Hindustan Standard dated 05 May 1951 reports: On 3 May 1951, R.S. Ruikar, in a statement endorsing a statement made by Phizu, the President of the Naga National Council and one of the chief advisers of Netaji in the I.N.A.'s historical march on Manipur. that "**the story of air-crash and Netaji's alleged death therein is a pure myth**", he said.

"All the evidence that has been placed before us, both by official and non-official sources leads us to the irresistible conclusion that **Netaji did not die in the air crash.**" Sri Phizu's statement Sri Ruikar added, made it preferably clear that Netaji is still alive and would return to India at an early date.'

In August 1952, the West Bengal Legislative Assembly unanimously adopted a non-official resolution expressing the view that the State Government should move the Government of India to take necessary steps for ascertaining "**the real facts about the alleged death of Netaji Subhas Chandra Bose.**" The resolution was moved by Dr Kanai Bhattacharjee, a member of the Forward Bloc, and supported by all the parties including the official Congress Party. The mover accepted an amendment of the Government Chief Whip deleting a suggestion to "set up a non-official enquiry committee" for the purpose.

Forward Bloc's claim of 'Netaji being alive' appeared again in October 1952: "**Netaji is alive and is somewhere in China or Russia**" -stated Mr. Sheel Bhadra Yajee, Chairman of Forward Bloc to pressman at Nagpur during the celebration of the Ninth Anniversary of the formation of the Azad Hind Government at Singapore.

Yajee stated that **his party was in touch with Netaji and the last occasion when a member contacted him was in July. Netaji would soon arrive in India**, he said. Yajee announced that the Forward Bloc would forge a united front with the newly formed Praja Socialist Party.

Pasumpon U. Muthuramalinga Thevar, who was disillusioned by the Congress leadership joined Bose's newly formed Forward Bloc in 1939. Beyond political advocacy, he was instrumental in rallying support for the I.N.A. led by Bose. His call to join the I.N.A. resonated across the southern districts of Madurai, Ramnad, Rameshwaram, Ramanathapuram, Sivaganga, Virudhunagar, Tuticorin and Tirunelveli and those spread across Burma (Myanmar), Singapore and Malaysia inspiring lakhs of men and women to enlist.

On 23 January 1949, in connection with the birthday anniversary celebrations of Bose, Thevar announced that Bose was alive and that he had met him. Soon thereafter Thevar disappeared without any explanation. He returned to public life in October 1950.

In 1955, internal divisions reappeared with the Forward Bloc. The Chairman Mohan Singh and Sheel Bhadra Yajee unilaterally declared the party merged into the Congress. Singh, Yajee, and their followers were expelled from the All India Forward Bloc and Thevar was elected Deputy Chairman of the party.

The very constitution of the 'Enquiry Committee' headed by Shah Nawaz Khan in 1956 itself was not approved by Thevar. Further, the 'Enquiry Committee' could not clarify the Government's position on whether Bose was declared a war criminal or not. Thevar understood the motive and denied speaking a single word on Netaji's whereabouts before the Committee.

In the Parliament, Thevar's nationalism manifested through his strong opposition to the special status accorded to Kashmir under Article 370, reflecting his vision for a United India without special provision.

CHAPTER NINE

Menon Sees Molotov

The Indian leadership repeatedly failed to realise Subhas Chandra Bose's foresight. The partnership of Allies from World War II collapsed swiftly as Bose thought. In the aftermath of the war, India became a zone for the US and Soviet competition for influence in the South Asian region.

Many events were taking place in the rapidly changing scenario in Kashmir. Sheikh Abdullah, President of the Kashmir National Conference was arrested on May 20 in connection with three speeches in furtherance of the Quit Kashmir movement said to be directed against the Maharaja. Abdullah preached sedition against the Maharaja and his family and accused him of being responsible for the violent movement in Kashmir.

Nehru was arrested in Kashmir for defying the ban on his entry while proceeding to Srinagar to arrange for Abdullah's defence. He was defended by Asaf Ali. The trial lasted for two and half months and Abdullah was sentenced to three years imprisonment and a fine of Rs. 1,500.

Bakshi Ghulam Mohammad, Acting President of the Kashmir National Conference, repudiated "most emphatically the bogey of Russian influence in Kashmir politics." He quoted the All-India States People's Conference, Jawaharlal Nehru, who said: "A few Communists have undoubtedly worked in Kashmir but it is absurd to think that the movement is due to them. It is still more absurd to think of Kashmir politics in terms of Azerbaijan."

Soon, the Amrita Bazar Patrika published a piece of sensational news on 15 September 1946 regarding Russian troop concentration on the Kashmir border.

Russian Troops On Kashmir Border?

Sensational Story In "Pratap"

'A sensational report of Russian troop concentration on the Kashmir border is contained in the local Vernacular Daily "Pratap" from the Srinagar correspondent. Basing its story on the alleged report of an officer of the Political Department, who recently retired and claiming him as an expert on Central Asiatic affairs, the "Pratap" front-pages it with sensational headlines **"Russian Troop Concentration On Kashmir Border"**. **"Government keeping strict vigilance on Central Asiatics in Srinagar"**.

According to the report, **Ghurki tribes belonging to Soviet Pamir under the command of Russians occupied Thagdambsh in Sikiang province and established their headquarters there**. The Chinese troops stationed there fled to Gilgit and Kashmir. The report adds that unidentified planes were flying on the same border.

The Royal Air Force is carrying on maneuvers, the report continues, to ascertain whether paratroops could be landed in Kashmir. The Army Intelligence Department, it says, has opened its office on the Kashmir border and the authorities are keeping strict vigilance on all inhabitants of Central Asia in Kashmir.'

"World War III is quite a possibility", said S.A. Dange, the prominent Trade Unioninst after returning from Moscow. There, he attended an International Trade Union Conference. "The next World War," he said will be a war between democratic and anti-democratic forces; the only question is when it will break out." The Russians might be forced to wage yet another war against anti-democratic imperialist forces. They blamed the United States, rather than Britain for the international tension, he added.

Russian Troops On Kashmir Border?

Sensational Story In "Pratap"

LAHORE, Sept. 12.

A sensational report of Russian troop concentration on Kashmir border is contained in the local Vernacular Daily "Pratap" from its Srinagar correspondent. Basing its story on the alleged report of an officer of the Political Department, who recently retired and claiming him as an expert on Central Asiatic affairs, the "Pratap" front-pages it with sensational headlines "Russian Troop Concentration On Kashmir Border". "Government keeping strict vigilance on Central Asiatics in Srinagar".

According to the report Ghurki tribes belonging to Soviet Pamir under command of Russian occupied Thagdambsh in Sikiang province and established their headquarters there. The Chinese troops stationed there fled to Gilgit and are under care of British forces. This resulted in the closing of roads for the British between Gilgit and Kashmir. The report adds that unidentified planes were seen flying on the same border.

The Royal Air Force are carrying on manoeuvres, the report continues, to ascertain whether paratroops could be landed in Kashmir. The Army Intelligence Department, it says, has opened its office on Kashmir border and the authorities are keeping strict vigilance on all inhabitants of Central Asia in Kashmir.—(U. P.)

He revealed that the Moscow Conference had entrusted him with the task of promoting trade unionism in South-East Asia countries. He said that the Government and the people of the Soviet Union were extremely sympathetic towards Indian aspirations. He added: "The trouble is that some of our own leaders are complicating the position by adopting an anti-Soviet attitude.

In October 1946, Generalissimo Stalin was accused of straining every nerve to get ready for a new war in a sensational article by Victor Kravchenko, the man who broke away from the Communist Party two years back. The former Chief Engineer and Director of Metallurgical Plants and Trust in Soviet Russia declared that "Not only does Stalin believe in the threat of a new war, but he and the Government he runs are straining every nerve to get ready for it. Their whole foreign and domestic policy confirms this."

"The main object of the fourth Five-Year Plan is to assure the increasing defensive capacity of the U.S.S.R. and to equip the armed forces of the Soviet Union with most up-to-date military techniques," he added.

After attending a Conference of the International Women's Domestic Federation in Moscow, a woman visitor was profoundly impressed and reportedly said that the people of Russia were keenly interested in Indian affairs and had goodwill for the Interim Government though they realised that India was not yet independent.

By then, the anti-Soviet attitudes of the top Indian leaders started changing rapidly. But was there any other reason behind Nehru's sudden interest in rapprochement with the Soviets at the time when the presence of Russian troops on the Kashmir border and Subhash Chandra Bose's presence in Frontier Province to meet the Faqir of Ipi was being simultaneously reported in the press?

On 28 September, it was reported that Mr. V. K. Kristina Menon, Secretary of the India Langue in London, who was in Paris as head of a special Mission from the Indian Interim Government had a two-hour interview with the Soviet Foreign Minister, V. M. Molotov, but refused to give any comment on leaving the Russian

Embassy. A spokesman for Mr. Menon said that his chief was **"seeing several other people"** before returning to London early next day.

Although Menon refused to comment on the nature of his talk, an Indian spokesman in close contact with him said earlier in the morning that the **discussion over highly secret matters could not and would not be disclosed. "There is no connection between Mr. Menon's interview and Peace Conference subjects,"** the spokesman said. He added that the meeting was to deal exclusively with Indian and Rusalan relations.

Pandit Jawaharlal Nehru selected Menon for the Mission to Molotov because of his Communist background the spokesman said (Menon was formerly a Communist Councillor for the London Borough of Saint Pancras). The spokesman said that the interview with the chief of the Russian Peace Conference Delegation had "been difficult to arrange" and that Menon would make a full report to Jawaharlal Nehru.

Informed quarters believed that the purpose of Menon's interview was to gain Soviet support for the new Indian Interim Government to offset, particularly in foreign relations, the predominant British influence.

Pandit Nehru sent his personal representative Menon to the General Assembly of the United Nations. **Menon had a 45-minute secret talk with Molotov**, at the Soviet Mansion at Glencove, Long Island, New York State.

Menon drove from the United Nations buildings at Flushing Meadow to the Soviet delegates' residence at the special invitation of Molotov and was shown over the building during his visit. **He talked at length to the Soviet Foreign Minister concerning his (Menon's) forthcoming visit to Moscow which he expects to make in December.**

It was learnt authoritatively that Menon would meet Molotov later at the General Assembly meeting. The meeting, it was understood would be a continuation of the Krishna Menon had with Molotov in Paris during the Foreign Ministers conference before Menon's visit to Moscow at the invitation of the Soviet Government.

Mr. Molotov had expressed his willingness to exchange diplomatic representatives with India, Jawaharlal Nehru, Vice-President of the Interim Government, stated amid cheers at the Central Legislative Assembly. It was proposed, he added, that the matter should be gone further in Moscow next month.

Pandit Nehru said Mr. V. K. Krishna Menon, formerly Secretary of the Pro-Congress India League in London, had been asked to meet various representatives of foreign Governments on Pandit Nehru's behalf to express India's desire to develop friendly relations, and he had seen Mr. Molotov in Paris.

Asked by a member of the Muslim League whether any party other than the head of the State could send such personal unofficial ambassadors on a diplomatic plane, Pandit Nehru said: "Obviously, it has been done by me."

The question of appointing Mr. Menon to explore the possibilities of establishing diplomatic relations with certain countries had been under consideration, Nehru added. In view of the food scarcity, however, India had sent a request directly to Moscow for wheat or rice.

The decision to send Mr. Menon was taken by him in consultation with all members of the Cabinet and the "Government of India chooses to function as far as possible as an independent Government," he said in reply to further questions.

MENON MEETS MOLOTOV AT PARIS

SPECIAL MISSION FROM INTERIM GOVT.

DISCUSSIONS OVER HIGHLY SECRET MATTERS

Interview Connected Exclusively With Indian & Russian Relations

Personnel Of Indian Delegation To UNO

Alternate Delegates & Also Advisers Selected

NEW DELHI, Sept. 28.—The composition of the Indian Delegation to the forthcoming session of the

The Amrita Bazar Patrika dated 31 October 1946 reports what M. Molotov said in the U.N.O General Assembly in New York: 'It is high time that the just demands of India were recognised. India is a member of the United Nations and under the Charter, her relationship with Britain should be based on sovereign equality,' said M. Molotov, the Soviet delegate, addressing the U.N.O. General Assembly, for the first time.

He further added: And yet have we not heard here India's appeal for support and assistance? We cannot turn a deaf ear to all this. Likewise, the Netherlands must recognise the justice of the demands of the people of Indonesia."

Giving a stern warning to the Atom Bomb diplomats, the Soviet Foreign Minister further added: 'One should not forget that an Atom Bomb on one side could possibly be answered by an Atom Bomb on the other side and, may be even by something else besides.'

Paul M. McGarr opines in 'A Serious Menace to Security': British Intelligence, V. K. Krishna Menon and the Indian High Commission in London, 1947–52 in the Journal of Imperial and Commonwealth History [pp 447]: 'Although committed to an early transfer of power, the Labour government's failure to advance a timetable for Indian self-government produced rumblings of discontent on the subcontinent. In February, with the illusion of British imperial power crumbling, the Royal Indian Navy mutinied in Bombay. The following month, with the internal situation in India threatening to spiral out of control, Attlee dispatched a cabinet mission to the subcontinent to negotiate terms for Britain's withdrawal. By 2 September, a transitional Indian government was in place, with Jawaharlal Nehru acting as its de facto premier and foreign minister. Eager to initiate contacts between his interim administration and European governments, Nehru asked Krishna Menon to serve as his unofficial ambassador-at-large. As Nehru's emissary, Menon called on the foreign ministries of Paris, Copenhagen, Oslo, and Stockholm. It was his meeting with the Soviet foreign minister, Vyacheslav Molotov in Paris in late September 1946, however, that rekindled British interest in Menon.

Stern Warning To Atom Bomb Diplomats

FLUSHING MEADOW (New York), Oct. 29.—'It is high time that the just demands of India were recognised. India is a member of the United Nations and under the Charter her relationship with Britain should be based on sovereign equality,' said M. Molotov, the Soviet delegate, addressing the U. N. O. General Assembly, for the first time.

He further added: 'And yet have we not heard here India's appeal for support and assistance? We cannot turn a deaf ear to all this. Likewise the Netherlands must recognise the justice of the demands of the people of I n d o n e s i a.''

Giving a stern warning to the Atom Bomb diplomats, the Soviet Foreign Minister further added: 'One should not forget that an Atom Bomb on one side could possibly be answered by an Atom Bomb on the other side and, may be even by something else besides.'

Molotov

Menon's meeting with Molotov had ostensibly been arranged to negotiate the sale of Soviet grain surpluses to India. Frederick Pethick Lawrence, Amery's successor as secretary of state for India, suspected that Menon's real agenda had been more sinister. As a fellow traveller, Pethick Lawrence argued, Menon had seized the first opportunity 'to make contact with, express sympathy with, and generally indicate India's desire to line up in the international field with, Russia rather than the 'Western bloc'.

But whether the disappearance of Subhash Chandra Bose and the information or claims about his whereabouts in Soviet Russia have anything to do with Soviet coming forward to aid India with food grains and strongly supporting India's causes as a member of the United Nations?

Quite interestinglyin *Charanik*'s notes, Bhagwanji says [16]: "*...Russia more a Shylock than U.S.A. in regard to aid. ...Russia is a more Shylock than the other party.*" It was rather intriguing for Bhagwanji to talk about the functioning of prisons camps in Siberia.

Declassified documents with the National Archives of India reveal sensational statements on Netaji Subhas Chandra Bose being in Soviet Russia:

An Indian Engineer of Calcutta, Mr. A. Sarkar, who is still alive and in Calcutta, made a statement to Calcutta Statesman saying that he met a German Jew, -Mr. B.A. Zerobin, Deputy Chief of the Plant, Machinosttroitelinizevod of Soviet Union. Mr. Sarkar was working in the Machine Building Plant at Gorlovska near the city of Doniest. He was working there being deputed by the Govt. of India. I also met Shri Sarkar in Calcutta and got the information that he received from Zerobin. I asked him why he didn't go to the press after returning to India. He told me that on receiving information about Netaji Subhas Chandra Bose from Zerobin, he approached the Indian Embassy in Moscow, but was warned by the Third Secretary of the Mission not to utter a word about it to anybody.

"Zerobin after being captured In Berlin, was taken in a train to an unknown place in the Siberian region, from where he was sent to a Re-orientation Camp somewhere in Siberia. **In that Camp one day he suddenly found Subhas Chandra Bose coming out of a Car, flanked by two Mongolian guards.** Seeing Bose, Zerobin excitedly rushed towards him and said: 'Sir, I have met you in Berlin.' **Bose replied in his characteristic style: 'Quite likely.' Bose then asked Zerobin: 'What are you doing here?'**Zerobin replied: 'I don't know what for.' Zerobin again asked Bose: 'What is your programme, Sir? Are you going back to India?' **Bose: "I expect it to be soon."**

While Bose and Zerobin were talking In German, (Bose knew German well) the Mongolian guards intervened: 'Not allowed.' Thereafter, Zerobin had no opportunity to meet Bose in the Siberian Re-orientation Camp.

Zerobin warned Mr. A.K. Sarkar that if he disclosed the report of Zerobin's meeting with Subhas Chandra Bose in the Re-orientation Camp in Siberia, the lives of both, Zerobin and Sarkar, would be seriously endangered. After retiring from the Govt. job, Shri Sarkar took the courage to disclose the report about Bose and that too many years later.

Prof Samar Guha requested the Prime Minister of India to take up the issue with the President of Russia to finally resolve the poignant question -what really happened to Netaji Subhas Chandra Bose -the Maha Kshatriya of Indian freedom? [Source: Declassified PMO Secret Political File: 870/11/P/10/93/Pol/Page 11-13]

Declassified documents [PMO Secret Political File No. 800/6/ C/3/88 -Pol] contain some sensational statements:

[1]

Mr. K.P.S. Menon's secret interview with the Russian Head of State Mr. Joseph Stalin:-

"Let not the people of India be swayed away by the interesting propaganda about the death or murder of Netaji Subhas Chandra Bose. He was not a prisoner in Russia. He was an honoured guest of

Stalin and living in a small village near "Magnitogarsk" in Russian Province ..." -K.P.S. Menon, 'Indian Life', Nov-Dec, 1953.'

[2]

"The mystery has further been heightened by the recent revelation in the so-long secret document of the then Govt. of India just published in London in the title "The Transfer of Power" pp 42-47. Mr. R.F. Mudie the then Home Member in the Viceroy's Executive Council, while replying to Mr. E.M. Jenkin's letter (Top secret No. 1157 dated August 11, 1945) regarding "Disposal of Bose" finally suggested (P 107, VOL VI):- **"Leave him where he is and don't ask for his surrender or release**", adding,"**he might, of course, in certain circumstances, be welcomed by the Russian.**"

[3]

Again, a Central intelligence department's confidential report submitted before both the commissions held that **Subhas Bose was in the Soviet Union under the assumed name of "GIZAI MILAN" a fact disclosed by the top Russian diplomats in Afghanistan and IRAN.** More facts may slowly come to light to dispel doubts about the death of the redoubtable revolutionary. -"BLITZ", JANUARY 21, 1978, PAGE -37.

According to a British intelligence report also, Subhas Chandra Bose was in Russia assuming the name *Ghilzai Malang. Ghilzai* is a dominant confederation among the Afghan tribal Pashtuns. In Afghanistan, it is said, the word *Malang* can be used for beggars to sufi saints to holy man and it is well known that Netaji was a past master in assuming false names.

CHAPTER TEN

Partition of India: The Betrayal

According to a declassified CIA document, as long ago as 1944, the Afghan Government suggested to the British that if India were to be granted Independence, the people of the NWFP and adjacent areas of Baluchistan should be allowed to determine their constitutional future. Upon the UK's announcement of the decision in 1947 to partition India into the dominions of Pakistan and India, the Afghan Government permitted a violent press and radio campaign for the creation of an Independent "Pathanistan." After the establishment of Pakistan and the inclusion of of the areas concerned in that dominion, Afghanistan demanded of the Government of Pakistan that complete autonomy be conceded to the areas by treaty between Governments of Pakistan and Afghanistan. While in control of India, the continued existence of the NWFP tribesmen as a distinct group was assured.

Abdul Ghaffār Khān also known as Bacha Khan or Badshah Khan was a Pashtun independence activist and founder of the Khudai Khidmatgar resistance movement against British colonial rule in India. The Khudai Khidmatgar's success and popularity eventually prompted the colonial government to launch numerous crackdowns against Khan and his supporters. The Khudai Khidmatgar experienced some of the most severe repression of the Indian independence movement.

Khān strongly opposed the proposal for the Partition of India into the Muslim-majority Dominion of Pakistan and the Hindu-majority Dominion of India, and consequently sided with the pro-union Indian National Congress and All-India Azad Muslim Conference against the pro-partition All-India Muslim League. When the Indian National Congress reluctantly declared its acceptance of the partition plan without consulting the Khudai Khidmatgar leaders, he felt deeply betrayed. In June 1947, Khan and other Khudai Khidmatgar leaders formally issued the 'Bannu Resolution' to the British authorities, demanding that the ethnic Pashtuns be given a choice to have an independent state of Pashtunistan, which was to comprise all of the Pashtun territories of British India and not be included (as almost all other Muslim-majority provinces were) within the state of Pakistan -the creation of which was still underway at the time.

However, the British government refused the demands of this resolution. In response, Khān and his elder brother, Abdul Jabbar Khān, boycotted the 1947 North-West Frontier Province referendum on whether the province should be merged with India or Pakistan, objecting that it did not offer options for the Pashtun-majority province to become independent or to join neighbouring Afghanistan. The Muslim League won an easy victory for Pakistan (289,244 votes against 2,874 for India).

After the Partition of India by the British government, Khān pledged allegiance to the newly created nation of Pakistan. He was frequently arrested by the Pakistani government between 1948 and 1954. In 1956, he was arrested for his opposition to the One Unit program, under which the government announced its plan to merge all the provinces of West Pakistan into a single unit to match the political structure of erstwhile East Pakistan. Khan was jailed or in exile for some years in the 1960s and 1970s.

Here is the "EXTRACTS FROM FRONTIER GANDHI'S AUTOBIOGRAPHY" collected from the Declassified SECRET PMO Political File No. 800/6/C/3/88 -Pol Record: PMO/1/247:

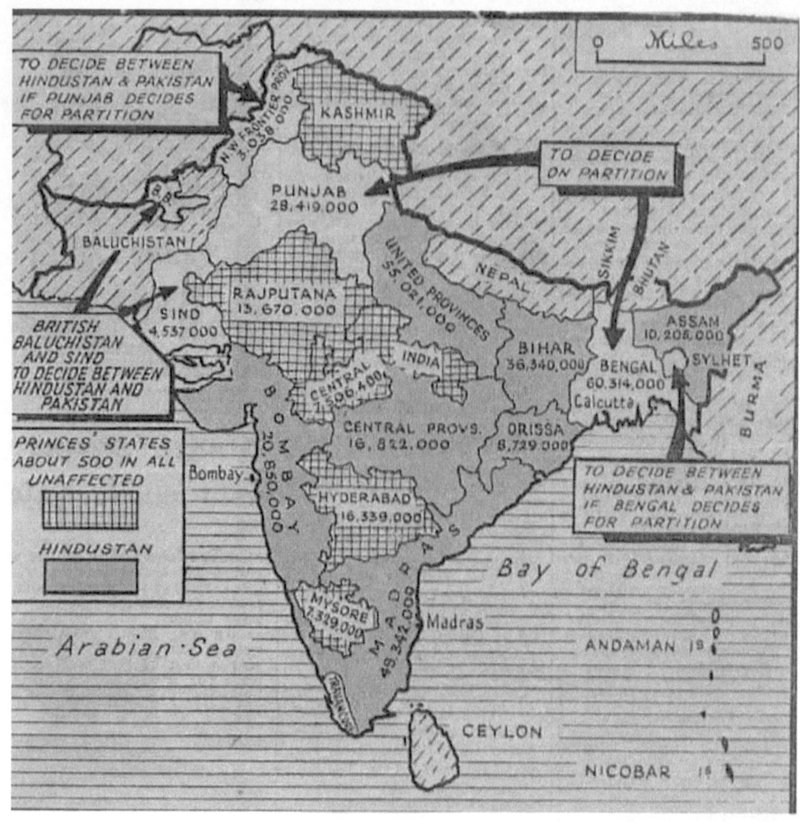

[Before split up of India in 1947]

PARTITION OF INDIA: FACTS REFLECT CONGRESS CULTURE

"I was not in favour of the elections of 1945-46. I thought that even if we won the elections, what good would it do if we could not work for the people? After all we did not want to win the elections or form a ministry for the sake of ruling over the people, but for the sake of serving them,

I attended the meeting of the Congress Working Committee and of the Parliamentary Board in Calcutta. After I had reported to Gandhiji on events and conditions in the Frontier Province, I told him that I did not want to take part in the elections. Gandhiji agreed with me. The Parliamentary Board tried to make me change my mind, but they did not succeed.

After the meeting of the Working Committee was over the people, I returned to my village and continued my work.

I saw British ladies going around canvassing too. They would go to people's homes, and, cleverly making use of the customs of exchanging & scarves when greeting a visitor, they would say "I have come to visit you, so you must give me a dupatta (scarf). But the dupatta I want is your vote." When I saw how hard and how enthusiastically these Britishers and their wives were working on behalf of the Muslim League, I changed my mind and decided that I would also take part in the campaign.

There was only one month to go before the elections. The issue at stake in this election of 1946- the last general election in United India was India or Pakistan, Hindu or Muslim, Islam or Kufr, temple or mosque.

The polling day came. The British wanted all out to help the Muslim League and hinder the Khudai Khidmatgars. But by the grace of God the Muslim League was defeated and we won the elections with a large majority. In July 1946 Maulana Azad and I were elected by the Khudai Khidmatgers and the Frontier Assembly to be members of the Central Assembly, the purpose of which was to give India a Constitution. The fact that we had secured such a clear majority in an election which was fought on very clear issues, and under conditions in which the government had allied itself with the Muslim League and had used all the Muslim leaders in India and all its power against us, could only mean one thing that the majority of people in the country were behind us.

When, therefore, in spite of all this, another referendum in 1947 was forced upon us, we considered this gross injustice and refused to have anything to do with such a referendum, we decided to boycott it so that the world might learn of the grass injustice that was to be inflicted upon us. Not only was the Viceroy's order for a new referendum illogical and unreasonable but it was also discriminating and partial. If the British meant this to be their parting gift to us, we did not accept it.

Whereas everywhere in India the representative Assenblion had been asked to decide whether they wanted to remain in India or go over to Pakistan, the North-West Frontier Province Assembly had not been given this right to choose This was an insult to the whole nation of the Pashtuns, which we could not under any circumstances tolerate. I must confess that It also hurt and grieved me deeply that even the congress working committee did not lift a finger to help us, as we had hoped they would. Tied hand and foot, they delivered us into the hands of our enemies.

Under these circumstances and after such treatment by the Congress, the question of whether I wanted to remain in India or go over to Pakistan is not only unnecessary but improper, because the Congress, which was the representative body in India not only deserted us but delivered us into the hands of our enemies. To meet them now is like killing all my Pathan self-respect, ethics, and traditions. The demand I made was that if the referendum was to be held at all it should be a referendum on the question of "Paktunistan or Pakistan" But nobody Listened to me and the referendum was forced upon us. As we refused to take part in this referendum the way was clear for the Muslim League, and they used all the cunning, deceit, and force they could command. In spite of all that they got only 50% of the votes, which is nowhere enough to decide the fate of a country or a nation.

On 3rd June 1947 Lord Mountbatton announced the Partition and the Congress and the Muslim League formally agreed to the creation of Pakistan. The Congress Government was a government in name only. Gandhiji and I were against partition, I cannot say what the other members felt about it, because I had not talked to them yet. But Sardar Patel and Rajagopalachari were in favour of partitions and they were putting pressure on others. The question of a referendum in the North-West Frontier Province was also discussed. Gandhiji and I were against the referendum too. I said there was no need at all for a referendum. Less than a year ago the election in the North-West Frontier Province had been fought on the issue of India or Pakistan. We had won this election with a large majority and the Muslim League had lost. *It was as simple* as that. Sardar Patel and Rajagopalachari did not see eye to eye with us on this question and they put a lot of pressure on the Working Committee and argued about the desirability of referendum at great length. Finally, the Working Committee agreed with them and voted in favour of both the partition of the country and the referendum. On this occasion, I told the Working Committee and Gandhiji that no Pathens were standing side by side with them in the struggle for the freedom of India and that we had made great sacrifices for the cause, but you are deserting us now," I told them and throwing us to the wolves. We held an election on the question of India or Pakistan, and we won this election with a large majority. Is there any doubt about what the Pakhtuns wanted? It was clear to the whole world.

Our people were very disappointed and a little annoyed too, I am afraid, because of this weakness on the part of Congress.That is why we said that if there was to be a referendum at all, it should be on the question of Pakhtunistan or Pakistan. After all, it was not we who had left the congress.The Congress had deserted us. If we had left the congress of our own accord, the British would have given us what we wanted, but we did not want to leave.I am convinced that, If the Congress had pressed this issue, if they had been as firm about it as they were about the question of Gurdaspur, or as firm as Jinnah was about this question, the British would have had to listen to them. We had great hopes from Jawaharlal, but I cannot understand why did he not do anything for us, the Pathans. When the Congress Working Committee agreed to the partition of the country and the referendum, I felt as if they had pronounced a death sentence on all the Pathans.I sat there, confounded and deeply distressed, Maulana Azad was sitting beside me. He advised me: "You ought to join the Muslim League now. It still makes me sad, and I still wonder what on path made him say a thing like that. For the Maulana had always been as much against the Muslim League's principles and practices as I was, and until then there was no evidence of any change in their policy which could have made it possible for us to become members. The Muslin League worked only for destruction, and I had devoted my whole life to construction. If the Maulana thought it was right for me to join the Muslim League, why had he not told me so before? Coming suddenly like this and at a time like this, his advice neither influenced nor impressed me. I can not change my beliefs and principles at a moment's notice, nor did I want my country and my people to change colour like a chameleon."

Abdul Gaffar Khān took the oath of allegiance to the new nation of Pakistan on 23 February 1948 at the first session of the Pakistan Constituent Assembly. However, suspicions of his allegiance persisted and under the new Pakistani government, Khān was placed under house arrest without charge from 1948 till 1954. In 1954, Khān split with his elder brother Khan Abdul Jabbar Khan (Dr Khan Sahib). In 1956 he was arrested for opposing the One Unit Scheme. The Pakistan government attempted in 1958 to reconcile with him and offered him a Ministry in the government, after the assassination of his brother, he however refused. He remained in prison till 1957 only to be re-arrested in 1958 until an illness in 1964 allowed for his release. He was conferred the 'Jawaharlal Nehru Award for International Understanding' by the Government of India in 1967.

The Dilemma of Maharaja Hari Singh

The nephew of Maharaja Pratap Singh, Maharaja Hari Singh, ascended to the throne of Jammu & Kashmir on September 23, 1925. During his rule, a number of progressive policies were implemented for the general welfare. His priorities remained the prohibition of untouchability, education, health, and women's empowerment. Hari Singh instituted several reforms, one of which was the reinforcement of the Jammu and Kashmir Tenancy Act 1923, which had been instituted by the previous government. He made sure Kashmir's landless peasant population received what was rightfully theirs. In an effort to enhance governance, Hari Singh also desired to reorganise the state bureaucracy. He began bringing in officials from other regions of British India, particularly Bengal, with this goal in mind. The reforms pleased the British as well.

The deeds of Singh, the last Dogra King, shaped Kashmir's past, present, and future, making him the most well-known and revered person in the Valley.

He was the son of Raja Amar Singh Jamwal, whose brother Pratap Singh ruled the state as king, and was born in Jammu on September 23, 1895. Following his father's death in 1909, the British became very interested in Hari Singh's academic pursuits. Singh received his primary education at the British-run Imperial Cadet Corps in Dehradun after attending Mayo College in Ajmer, Rajasthan. After his uncle Pratap Singh died in 1925, Singh, at thirty years old, succeeded to the title of Maharaja of J&K.

A history professor and the head of the Institute of Kashmir Studies in Srinagar, Dr. M.Y. Ganie, told 'The Print' that Hari Singh's entry signaled a significant shift in the Dogra dynasty. The lecturer recounted how his own uncle, Ghulam Hasan Ganie, who worked in the Dogra administration, would frequently discuss the responsibility of institutions operating under the Dogra system.

"Hari Singh made a number of decisions after ascending to the throne. Hari Singh established laws requiring children to attend what became known as Jabri schools in order to obtain a modern education." Jabar denotes force, according to Professor Ganie.

Hari Singh instituted several reforms, one of which was the reinforcement of the Jammu and Kashmir Tenancy Act 1923, which had been instituted by the previous government. Ganie claimed that Singh made sure Kashmir's landless peasant population received justice.

In an effort to enhance governance, Hari Singh also desired to reorganize the state bureaucracy. He began bringing in officials from other regions of British India, particularly Bengal, with this goal in mind. The reforms pleased the British as well. According to Ganie, Singh's overall government was praiseworthy. However, Singh's efforts were forgotten.

Many people in the state, like Ganie Choudhary, tend to view the former Dogra king's benefits. According to these opinions, Hari Singh was superior than his forerunners. However, the vast majority of people in the Valley tend to disagree, frequently refusing to even compare Hari Singh to his forebears or only placing the blame on him for his actions before to 1947 as well as the current standoff in Kashmir.

Dogras, under the able military authority of Gulab Singh and General Zorawar Singh, established the Jammu and Kashmir kingdom by expanding its boundaries up to the border of Russia in the North and Tibet in the East and remained the largest priceley state in British India up to 1947, when India attained freedom. Dogra dynasty ruled Ladakh, Gilgit-Baltistan, Muzaffarabad-Mirpur, Aksai Chin, and Saksham valley and were de facto rulers of feudatories like Hunza and Nagar.

A popular uprising against Hari Singh began in 1931 when Abdul Qadeer of Swat (modern-day Pakistan), an employee of an English army officer, was put on trial for treason and conspiracy to overthrow the regime. Records suggested 24 Kashmiri people were killed in that summer. The uprising against Hari Singh had begun and to date, July 13 is remembered as Martyrs' Day across the Valley.

Though Hari Singh largely contained the rebellions between 1931 and 1947, his real test came with the partition of British India. Hari Singh, backed by his administration, wanted J&K to remain an independent region, espoused by his Prime Minister Ram Chandra Kak, historians said.

Hari Singh even signed a Stand Still Agreement with Pakistan to maintain the status quo till the final decision on Kashmir was agreed upon. India, however, did not sign the agreement. In the meantime, people from Chenab Valley's Poonch region, in June 1947, raised arms against Hari Singh's Dogra soldiers even as the subcontinent was engulfed with communal riots.

Hari Singh, who had till then successfully maneuvered his way between India and Pakistan to remain independent, was caught in a fix. The rebellion in the Poonch region of J&K followed by a brutal crackdown by Singh's forces. For long, the Indian state maintained that the tribal militias were Pakistani troopers.

After India got Independence, the political class in Jammu and Kashmir often tried hard to downplay the contribution of the Dogra dynasty vilifying the warriors from the royal house, but Maharaja Hari Singh, the last Dogra ruler of the erstwhile state is considered an icon among the youth in the region.

However, the Partition of 1947 began dismantling the legacy of Maharaja Gulab Singh, and soon after when invaders forcibly occupied the region of Gilgit-Baltistan and Mirpur, Muzaffarabad the proud achievements of the Dogra dynasty receded to the pages of history. Under pressure, Hari Singh signed the Instrument of Accession to join India. He allowed Indian troops in Kashmir to defend the region and the insurgency in Poonch.

Hari Singh remained the titular Maharaja of J&K even after he was made to appoint his son as the President or Sadr-e-Riyaasat of the state. Sheikh Abdullah was appointed the Prime Minister of J&K. People from the Dogra community in Jammu-Kashmir and around take pride in the legacy and part of their forefathers in shaping Jammu and Kashmir, that it is today.

CHAPTER TWELVE

Former INA Commanders Led Attack On Kashmir

A spokesman of the Pakistan Government said on the night of October 29, 1947: "It may be taken for granted that the Government of Pakistan will refuse to accept an accession... ." A small force of Indians -reportedly two companies of Sikhs met the invaders about 30 miles from the Kashmir capital of Srinagar and after losing several men including a company commander retreated to prepared defence lines 26 miles from the capital. The invading Army which was equipped with artillery, machineguns, and transport included some members of Subhas Chandra Chandra Bose's Indian National Army. Sources said some invaders and officers were members of the provisional government of independent India which attacked the British forces along the Imphal -Kohima border during the Second World War.

Indian Army troops flown to relieve Kashmir retreated before thousands of well-armed insurgents who crossed into the state when Kashmir decided to join the Dominion of India.

On October 31, it was reported that Pakistan irregulars armed with machine guns, mortars, and artillery drove within 19 miles of Srinagar in a four-pronged drive that threatened to engulf the Kashmir capital in a matter of days.

Reportedly led by Generals Kiani, and Habib ur Rahaman -former followers of the Provisional Government of Azad Hind of Netaji Subhas Chandra Bose, the raiders drove Indian Union Troops from Barmoola and swept on towards Srinagar's airdrome through which Hindu reinforcements were being funneled.

It was understood that when Jinnah heard that Kashmir had joined the Indian Union and Indian troops were being sent to the State, he phoned General Gracey, acting Chief of the Pakistan Army to move troops into Pakistan, but Gracey replied it would be tantamount to an act of war because Kashmir has become part of India. Mr. Jinnah insisted whereupon Field Marshal Sir Claude Auchinleck flew to Lahore and threatened he and every other British officer would resign if Pakistan troops invaded Kashmir.

The correspondent added Mr. Jinnah was thus compelled to stay his hand, but his complicity in the attack by the tribal raiders continued. The new invasion plan in execution was reported to be drafted by Sheikh Hamid, Pakistan's Chief of Staff who was formerly Auchinleck's Private Secretary.

The London Daily Telegraph also reported that former Indian National Army Generals like Habibur Rahman and M.Z. Kiani who was with Netaji Subhas Chandra Bose till the last moment was now commanding the Pakistani insurgents in Kashmir. They were some of the most loyal and dedicated INA officers of Bose who left India after the partition.

Major General Mohammed Zaman Kiani

Mohammad Zaman Kiani was born in the village of Tyal, near Bara Kahu in the Rawalpindi District, now part of Islamabad, Pakistan. He was an officer of the British Indian Army. In March 1941 the 1st Battalion 14th Punjab Regiment was sent to Malaya and Mohammed Zaman Kiani fought in the Battle of Malaya during World War II and was taken prisoner of war. He later joined the First Indian National Army, when it was formed in 1942 under the command of Mohan Singh. After this army collapsed due to disagreements with the Japanese, the Indian Independence League placed Kiani as Army Commander of the remains, with Jagannath Rao Bhonsle as Director of the Military Bureau.

After the arrival of Subhas Chandra Bose in 1943 and the revival of the Indian National Army, as well as the proclamation of the Free India government, Kiani was appointed the commander of the first division, which he led in 1944. At the time of the fall of Rangoon, Kiani led the personnel of the Indian National Army and the Azad Hind Government who, along with Bose, marched to Bangkok. Bose, as the Head of the State, Provisional Government of Azad Hind, ordered on 16th August 1945: "During my absence from Syonan, Major General M.Z. Kiani will represent the Provisional Government of Azad Hind." Bose entrusted Kiani to be the Chairman of an eight-member Committee to deal with all affairs connected with the Provisional Government of Azad Hind.

Kiani, however, was captured by the British 5th Division at Singapore on 25 August 1945 as the commander of the I.N.A., along with the rest of his troops. He was repatriated to India and interned until 1946, before being cashiered and discharged from the British Indian Army.

Following the Partition of India, Kiani returned to Rawalpindi. In September 1947, Pakistani Prime Minister Liaquat Ali Khan and Punjabi Minister Shaukat Hayat Khan put him in charge of the southern wing of Pakistan's effort to overthrow the Maharaja of Jammu and Kashmir.

General Kiani established a General Headquarters, GHQ Azad, based in Gujrat City. From there, his forces organised raiding operations on the Kashmir border and directed the Kashmiri rebels in Poonch, eventually leading to the formation of Azad Kashmir. Brigadier Habibur Rehman served as his chief of staff. He served as Pakistan's political agent to Gilgit in the late 1950s.

Colonel Habibur Rahman

Habibur Rahman, son of Raja Manzoor Ahmad Khan was born in the village of Panjeri, Mirpur District in Jammu and Kashmir. Mohan Singh was from the same unit from which was Rahman and was his close friend. In February 1942, Rahman decided to join the Indian National Army. He was another army officer in the I.N.A. who was charged with "waging war against His Majesty the King Emperor". He served as Bose's chief of staff in Singapore. Towards the end of 1944, Bose gave Rahman the command of the 4th Guerrilla Regiment also called the Nehru Brigade. His regiment distinguished itself on the battlefield. Rangoon fell during the last week of April. Bose's trusted Adjutant Rahman was taken prisoner by Allied forces and later repatriated to India.

Naeemur-Rahman, son of Habib ur Rahman, who resides in Islamabad, claims that his father told him that he had accompanied Netaji on a visit to Tokyo two or three months before the alleged crash in course of such a meeting had taken place between Netaji and Soviet Ambassodor in Tokyo to finalise plans of the proposed trip to Russia. [Declassified PMO Political File No. 870/11/P/16/92/POL]

After Independence, Muhammad Ali Jinnah was delighted with Rahman joining the government service and advised him in writing to visit and report about the current situation of the state of Jammu and Kashmir in Srinagar. Following this request, he went to visit the Prime Minister of Jammu & Kashmir Ram Chandra Kak and Maharaja Hari Singh to better understand their views on the State of Jammu and Kashmir joining Pakistan.

Rahman played an important role in the First Kashmir War. He joined Major General Zaman Kiani, in launching a rebellion against the Maharaja from Gujrat in Pakistani Punjab. Rahman and his volunteer force launched an attack on the Bhimber town. However, the records of the 11th Cavalry of the Pakistan Army indicate that their efforts did not succeed, and eventually, the Cavalry was responsible for conquering Bhimber.

In 1947, Rahman tried his level best to organise the ex-army people to wrest control of Jammu and Kashmir. He led many battles against the Dogra forces, particularly in Bhimber and Kotli. Under the leadership of Rahman, the Muslims of Bhimber rose against the Dogra rulers and separated Bhimber from the state of Jammu & Kashmir.

A GHQ Azad (General Headquarters of Azad Kashmir) was formed in Gujrat, Pakistan, with General Zaman Kiani as the commander-in-chief and Habibur Rahman as the chief of staff.

In 1966 when a Japanese biographer of Netaji, Mr. Hayashida, met Habibur in Rawalpindi, he repeated nothing than the same story of Netaji's death but added: 'Netaji Subhas Chandra Bose was the greatest revolutionary that the Indian Subcontinent produced in the present century... Many in Bharat still believe that he is still alive and will turn up someday. How we wish he had come back alive! The flame of freedom lit by him is still burning and will continue to inspire the freedom fighters all over the world for all times to come.' [Declassified PMO Political File No. 870/11/P/16/92/POL]

Lt. Col. Taj Muhammad Khanzada

Said to be part of the Special Service Group (Commandos) of the I.N.A.-Led Rawalpindi Sector of GHQ Azad under Major General Zaman Kiani -responsible for supporting operations by Pakistani irregulars, and the army in Poonch.

Lt. Col. Burhan-ud-Din

Son of the then king of Chitral Shuja ul-Mulk, ruler of Chitral in Gilgit-Baltistan. During the battle of Singapore in February 1942 he was a Lieutenant serving with "B" Company. He was taken prisoner of war at the fall of Singapore in February 1942. After being taken prisoner of war he volunteered for the Indian National Army. By 1944, Burhan-ud-Din was one of three IOCs of the Indian National Army.

When Rangoon fell to the British on 3 May 1945, Burhan-ud-Din was captured the same day and placed under arrest. He was charged with a wartime atrocity. Many men under his command had often left their posts to go into Rangoon in search of women, often not to return for several days. Burhan-ud-Din was offended by this practice, so he had five of his soldiers rounded up in Rangoon, brought back, and flogged as deserters. One of them, whose name was Joga Singh, died during the flogging. Burhan-ud-Din was ultimately tried in a Military Court. Brigadier Kodandera M. Cariappa's court sentenced Burhan to seven years of rigorous imprisonment in 1946. It was stated in the charge sheet that Burhan-ud-Din had waged war against the King.

Burhan and his co-convicts were released on 13 August 1947 and their sentences were nullified. After his release, he immediately returned to Chitral. Burhan-ud-Din led Chitral troops to support the British-manufactured rebellion of Gilgit Scouts. Helped to secure Gilgit and Astore.

For his role in capturing Chilas, he was given the title "Fateh-i-Chilas" by the Pakistan Government. But, that didn't stop him from signing "Lieutenant Shahzada Burhanuddin, 1st Squadron, Indian Air Force" in the guest book at Mauripur Air Base at Karachi in 1966, immediately after the 1965 war with India.

The Siege of Skardu was a prolonged military blockade carried out by the Gilgit Scouts, Chitral Scouts, and Chitral State Bodyguards, acting in coordination against Jammu and Kashmir State Forces and the Indian Army in the town of Skardu in 1947.

Major Mata-Ul-Mulk

Brother of Burhan-ud-Din, educated at the Prince of Wales Royal Indian Military College -served as a captain in World War II at Malaya & Singapore in 1941. After the surrender, he was made Prisoner of War. He also headed the Chitral Body Guard Force in 1946 as Colonel and participated in the capture of Skardu. He was made Prisoner of War again, arrested, and imprisoned in Peshawar from 1948-1950.

Major Malik Munawar Khan Awan

Munawar was born in Chakwal District, Punjab, British India. He joined the British Army and was deployed at Rangoon. After the fall of Rangoon, he was captured by the Japanese along with his fellow soldiers. In prison, Lieutenant Munawar quickly picked up the Japanese language and even the Japanese saw the potential in the young man. They moved him out of the prison camp and enlisted him in the Imperial Japanese Army, where he received special training.

Lieutenant Munawar rebelled against the British Crown along with other Muslim, Hindu, and Sikh Officers and joined the Indian National Army movement of Bose and fought against British Troops commanding the 1st Battalion of the 2nd Guerilla Regiment of I.N.A. He fiercely fought against the Allied forces in the Battle of Imphal, and inflicted heavy causalities of men & material but was later captured by the Allied forces. He was given on death sentence for his defiance of the British Crown. Captain Munawar Awan was freed, along with other I.N.A. prisoners, when the Partition of India occurred. He moved to Pakistan and was invited to join the Pakistan Army by Prime Minister Liaquat Ali Khan. He then joined the Azad Kashmir Regular Forces (AKRF), which later became the Azad Kashmir Regiment.

During his two-month stay in occupied Kashmir, he wiped off seven Indian Infantry Battalions during seventeen Battles/ Encounters with the Indian Army. He established his Government, appointed his own administrative staff, and hoisted the Pakistani Flag on all official buildings of captured areas till Cease Fire. It was the capture of this vast area by Major Munawar Khan that served as the basis of Operation Grand Slam to capture Akhnor, adjacent to Rajouri and thus cutting India from the rest of Kashmir.

Operation Gibraltar was launched in July 1965 with the aim of Pakistani infiltration of Jammu & Kashmir. Awan, who now held the rank of major, was involved in this, leading troops in heavy fighting at a pass near Rajouri. After the Tashkent Agreement between India and Pakistan, he was ordered to withdraw his forces and return to Rawalpindi.

Lt. Col. Raja Mohammed Arshad

He was I.N.A.'s highest-ranking staff officer, posted as GSO I, during the Imphal-Kohima campaign. After partition, he remained in Pakistan, commanded the "Azad Kashmir Force" in the Mirpur sector,

Like there are suggestions that some I.N.A. veterans led Pakistani irregulars during the First Kashmir War, some accounts also suggest that the **I.N.A. veterans were involved in training civilian resistance forces against the Nizam's Razakars before the execution of Operation Polo and the annexation of Hyderabad.**

In October 1947, the Pakistan Government's accusations that ex-INA troops had attacked Muslim villages in Pakistan were denied by Maharaja Hari Singh. On the contrary, it was reported, that "people in their thousands from Pakistan armed with modern weapons were raiding Ponch territory inside Kashmir."

In Pakistan, many ex-I.N.A. officers reportedly participated in the 1947-48 Kashmir war but this operation was conducted outside the normal chain of command of the army. **Three years later, the ex-I.N.A. soldiers who participated in Kashmir operations in 1947-48, were involved in a coup within the Pakistan army. Several officers were arrested for the conspiracy to overthrow the civilian government. Most of these officers had participated in Kashmir operations.**

Mr. Liaquat Ali Khan, the Prime Minister of Pakistan in his broadcast from Lahore on the night of November 4, 1947 counter charged: "After the massacre of Muslims in the East Punjab, and the East Punjab States, the forces of annihilation turned on Jammu and Kashmir. **Towards the end of September, the I.N.A. and the Rashtriya Sevak Sangh shifted their headquarters from Amritsar to Jammu and thousands of so-called Sikh refugees came from the East and not the West Punjab. They came armed with modern weapons and were provided with more weapons by the State authorities.** They set about their formal business in Jammu and Poonch repeating the horrible drama that they had enacted in

East Punjab. .."

"The declared object of the Indian Government is to strengthen the Maharaja's hand. How bloodstained these hands are is quite well-known to the leaders of India even though they have chosen to forget this fact now."

On November 26, 1947, replying to questions in the Constituent Assembly, Defence Minister Sardar Baldev Singh said the India Government was considering the feasibility of appointing suitable officers of Netaji's Indian National Army for posts in the Indian Army. No attempt was made so far to appoint anyone of the I.N.A. men in the Indian Army presently,

In the early stages of the Srinagar Valley fighting, it was reported that Major General M. Z. Kiani of I.N.A. was in general control of the raiders, but the India Government was unable to substantiate it, said Baldev Singh, adding "The Government of India are aware other I.N.A. men are also taking part in the raiders' camps against Indian and Kashmir forces, but the Government is unable to verify such reports."
Baldev Singh said the Indian army constituted after the partition of India was sufficient for peacetime purposes though he refused to divulge details of the composition of the Indian Army.

On 7 September 1951, the Deputy Defence Minister of India said in Parliament that the number of I.N.A. officers and other ranks gone to Pakistan was not known to the Government of India as re-enrolment in the I.N.A. was not permissible prior to 1948. Maj. Gen. Himatsinghji, Deputy Minister said that seven officers, 6 JCOs, 24 NCOs, and 1010 other ranks belonging to ex-I.N.A. had been enrolled in India's land forces.

When questions were asked, "In view of the clenched fist shown against India by Pakistan and in view of the war propaganda by Pakistan do the Government propose to recruit more I.N.A. officers and men in the regular army? If not why not?", Prime Minister Jawaharlal Nehru replied, "No, because it has no relevance."

He further replied that it was clearly a well-known fact that some ex-I.N.A. officers played a leading part in the operation against Kashmir from Pakistan. They were not then recruited as regulars in the Pakistan Army but there was only a "thin veil."

In his *FROM MY BONES*, Col. Gurbaksh Singh Dhillon of I.N.A. writes: "No wonder, that in a statement published in The Statesman dated 4th March 1946, Pandit Jawaharlal Nehru revealed that Shah Nawaz, Sahgal and (Dhillon) -the three I.N.A. officers, were not released owing to demonstrations in India, but the Indian Army had demanded their release.

What an irony that when Nehru came into power, the I.N.A. soldiers were not taken back into the Indian Army!"
On 02 November 1947, it was reported that Major General Zaman Kiani and Captain Abdul Rasheed were fighting among "raiders" in Kashmir which created surprise and sorrow among the local I.N.A. men. They expressed their regret that the circumstances should have led them into the arms of reaction.
However, a senior I.N.A. officer pointed out that this should be a lesson to the national leadership. While the Nehru Government refrained from lifting the ban from I.N.A. Joining the army and men like General Mohan Singh, General Bhonsle, and Dhilon were not trusted for an army Job, the Leaguers had risked arming the ex-Azad Hind Fauj personnel.
The training of I.N.A. men and their patriotism should have been fully utilised in Kashmir by the Indian Government. Even though some of their ex-colleagues were on the other side, they were more competent to fight for India than the army men, under Auchinleck.

It is interesting to note that at that time even the U.P. Government had not lifted the ban on the I.N.A. personnel from joining the armed constabulary. If the ex-I.N.A. men had no place in the Indian Army and were well accepted by the Pakistan Government, they were only doing their duties.

Afterall after the defeat of the Japanese in the Second World War, Netaji Subhas Chandra Bose disbanding I.N.A., urged the

Army men to stay positive and keep doing what best they could do for the nation. In his talking on Warcraft to his men, he said, "Soldiers who always remain faithful to their nation, are always prepared to sacrifice their lives, are invincible." However, the India Government was unable to substantiate it.

CHAPTER THIRTEEN

Open The Way To Kashmir

[Pashtun tribesmen from Waziristan bound for Kashmir, 1947]

It is not true that Pakistan lent support to the tribal infiltration because it had been precipitated by an internal revolt of the Muslim population of the region. The argument that peasant unrest in Poonch (June to October 1947) triggered a large-scale revolt of the

Muslims against the Hindu ruler is untenable -an argument made by Prof. Nandalal Chakrabarti, former Head of the Department of Political Science, Presidency College, Kolkata was published in the 'The Statesman, January 14, 2019.

It reads: "On the evening of 24 October 1947, at a dinner party in Delhi, Nehru informed Mountbatten that an invasion of Kashmir by tribesmen from the North West Frontier had taken place. Apprehending imminent danger, the Viceroy called a meeting of the Defence Committee next morning. General Lockhart, Commander-in-Chief of the Indian Army, reported based on a communication from the Pakistan Army Headquarters in Rawalpindi, that 5000 tribesmen from the North West had entered Kashmir and burnt down the town of Muzaffarabad on their way towards Srinagar. Maharaja Hari Singh, the ruler of Kashmir, made a desperate appeal for help to India. He wrote to Mountbatten on 26 October that tribesmen could not have come in motor trucks using the Mansehra-Muzaffarabad Road fully armed with up-to-date weapons without the knowledge of the Provisional Government of the North West Frontier Province and the Government of Pakistan. Retired officers of the Pakistan Army confirmed that Pakistan had provided logistic support to the tribesmen.

Following the division of the British Indian Army, the bulk of the military assets remained within the Dominion of India in 1947. Those within the Dominion of Pakistan were largely obsolete. How did Pakistan supply modern arms and ammunition to the tribesmen? It is not true that Pakistan lent support to the tribal infiltration because it had been precipitated by an internal revolt of the Muslim population of the region. The argument that peasant unrest in Poonch (June to October 1947) triggered a large-scale revolt of the Muslims against the Hindu ruler is untenable. General Victor Scott, the British Commander-in-Chief of the Kashmir state forces, informed that "in September 1947, the State troops had escorted one lakh Muslims through Jammu territory on their way to Pakistan and an equal number of Sikhs and Hindus going the other way" (General Victor Scott's Report; British Library). Thus, the raiders' objective had hardly anything to do with the bogey of Muslims in danger in Kashmir, a convenient ruse that is proffered by Pakistan to cover up its own agenda of territorial expansion.

What happened in Kashmir in 1947? In the wake of Partition, when communal tension flared up around the state, Hindu-Muslim relations became strained in certain areas. There was unease in Jammu and the frontier adjoining the Pathan tribal areas. And yet, "Kashmir", as stated by the British Resident W P Webb, "remained free from communal disturbances". The region had never allowed the rot to set in despite the instigation of communal outfits from within and outside. As early as 1943, the Muslim League envoy to Kashmir informed Jinnah, "No important religious leader has ever made Kashmir his home or even an ordinary centre of Islamic activities. It will require considerable effort, spread over a long period of time, to reform them and convert them into true Muslims".

Three years later, Agha Saukat Ali, a Muslim Conference leader in Kashmir, threatened "direct action" to enforce the two-nation agenda but, failed to unite the warring factions of the Muslim Conference. This proves that there was no communal sentiment. Pakistan and its cohorts propagated the view that the tribesmen, driven by their primordial greed and cruel instinct for destruction, looted the state. Sharbaz Khan Mazari, a tribal leader from Baluchistan, in his book A journey to disillusionment, says that he was stopped by Pakistani officials while trying to persuade some men to join the fighting in Kashmir.

As Mazari points out, they thought that "he and his men were intent on partaking in the plunder that was taking place". The reference to the people unleashing the plunder has been made vague and if we go by his own statement, the intention of Mazari and his people was different. Did the Pakistani officials want to hide from the Baluch tribal leader what the military contingent of Pakistan was doing inside Kashmir, to capture the entire region? If it is taken for granted that the tribesman was the saviour of the distressed Muslim brethren, the question remains unresolved as to how the saviour became the looter. Attempts to explain it by citing the greedy and cruel nature of the tribes of the North West have never been convincing. Obviously, they were driven by a motive unrelated to Pakistan's plan of action.

Satya Bakshi, a renowned journalist and a freedom fighter wrote in an editorial in *"Socialist Republican"* on 8 November 1947 that INA men like Major General M.Z. Kiani and Col Habibur Rehman had led the tribesmen into the State of Jammu and Kashmir. Pakistani sources also recorded ex-INA officers' involvement in the raid. V. P. Menon, the constitutional advisor to Mountbatten, in the magnum opus, Integration of the Indian States", referred to the presence of INA veterans like Md Zaman Kiani and Burhanuddin in the tribal raid. The presence of Burhanuddin makes the entire episode more intriguing. Burhanuddin was the Prince of Chitral who became a Commander of INA in Burma. Chitral, the largest district in the Khyber Pakhtunkhwa previously known as North West Frontier Province, is separated from Tajikistan by a narrow strip of the Wakhan Corridor, which extends from north-eastern Afghanistan to China. According to a British intelligence report of 1946, Nehru received a letter from Bose stating he was in Russia and that he wanted to come to India via Chitral (File No. 223 INA).

Did Burhanuddin have any inkling of the plan? It has often been pointed out that Burhanuddin joined the raid because he endorsed Kashmir's accession to Pakistan and supported a Muslim uprising against the ruler of Kashmir, Maharaja Hari Singh, who was inclined towards accession to India. There was speculation too that since he had a strong Islamic orientation, he must have organised the raid with Kiani to free his Muslim brethren from Hindu rule. Nothing can be farther from the truth. On the other hand, if it is argued that Kiani organised the raid because after migrating to Pakistan he was put in charge of the southern wing to overthrow the Government of Jammu and Kashmir, it would only be a half truth. Kiani did not willingly leave India. He left India because he felt the worst possible disgrace. This will be evident from the Congress leaders' attitude towards the INA.

In an interview with a returned POW, Captain Hari Badhwar on 18 October 1945, Asaf Ali, a member of the Congress Working Committee, said that if the Congress was in power "it would have no hesitation in removing all INA from services" and "if Government now postponed trials, the Congress would put INA leaders on trial when in power". Everybody knows who came to power in India in 1947 and how INA soldiers/ officers were prevented from joining the Indian Army despite cosmetic changes of policy from time to time. They were welcomed by Pakistan and offered opportunities to join the forces. But it would be a gross over-simplification to infer that they opted for the other Dominion. One should not ignore their constraints in India. They would not have been allowed to organise forces to move towards Kashmir for receiving their leader. Neither the British nor the Indian authorities accorded them any locus standi. So, it could have been very much on the cards that these people had an underlying motive different from occupation of Kashmir by Pakistan.

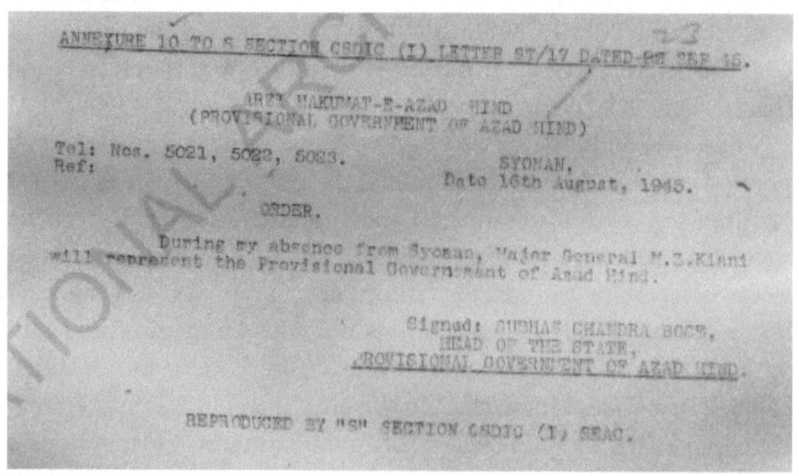

ANNEXURE 10 TO S SECTION CSDIC (I) LETTER ST/17 DATED 28 SEP 45.

ARZI HAKUMAT-E-AZAD HIND
(PROVISIONAL GOVERNMENT OF AZAD HIND)

Tel: Nos. 5021, 5022, 5023.
Ref:
SYONAN,
Date 16th August, 1945.

ORDER.

During my absence from Syonan, Major General M.Z.Kiani will represent the Provisional Government of Azad Hind.

Signed: SUBHAS CHANDRA BOSE,
HEAD OF THE STATE,
PROVISIONAL GOVERNMENT OF AZAD HIND.

REPRODUCED BY "S" SECTION CSDIC (I) SEAC.

[Declassified File No. 75/INA/Page: 3]

It is preposterous to assume that Major General Kiani, who was instructed by Subhas Chandra Bose himself to represent the Provisional Government of Azad Hind in his absence, would organise the raid to assist Pakistan's annexation of Kashmir. Whatever have been the front, in all likelihood these men masterminded the raid, receiving the information of Bose's possible return to India through that region. An intelligence report of the Home Department reveals that in 1946 meetings were held in the Northwest Frontier Province demanding release of all INA men from custody.

INA's connection with the North-West Frontier is not, therefore, a figment of imagination. Bose himself planned attacks on British forces from the tribal areas of the North-West. He stated in his memorandum of 9 April 1941 presented in Germany, that "**our agents are already working in the independent Tribal territory lying between Afghanistan and India. Their efforts will have to be coordinated and an attack on British military centres will have to be planned on a large scale**". (File No L/P and J/ 12/217: Public Record Office, London). Bhagatram Talwar, one of Bose's aides, brought Sodhi Harminder Singh and Santimoy Ganguly from India in the same year for training in underground combat in Afghanistan. Such circumstantial evidence suggests that the ex-INA men tried to facilitate their leader's safe passage to Kashmir by leading the tribesmen to the Valley to establish a completely free zone there."

Dr. Madhusudan Pal quotes some vital documents on the tribal invasion of Kashmir in his book [12]: *The Great Divide Britain, India and Pakistan* [pp 441 & 474] by H. V. Hodson reveals: '...In September and October events of some importance were taking place in Kashmir, but the Government of India was too preoccupied, first with Punjab...

...On the evening of Friday 14th October. The Governor General and the Foreign Minister of Siam were guests of Pandit Nehru at dinner at the latter's house in New Delhi. During the evening Lord Mountbatten was taken aside by his host, who told him that news had come in of a large scale invastion of tribesmen from North-West-Frontier into Kashmir. Realising at once that a new and grave situation has arisen, Lord Mountbatten called a special meeting of the Defence Committee at 11 A.M. next morning. There an official report was received from General Lockhart, Commander-in-Chief Indian Army who had been informed by Headquarters, Pakistan Army, in Rawalpindi that some 5,000 tribesmen had entered Kashmir three days previously from the West and had seized and burnt the town of Muzaffarabad on their way towards Srinagar.'

'Lord Mountbatten saw Mr. Liaquat Ali Khan alone and told him he had been criminally foolish thus once again to jeopardise the chance of any negotiations. Having rebuked one party he was able to placate the other to the point of persuading Pandit Nehru to meet Liaquat Ali Khan at 4 O'oclock that afternoon.

Pandit Nehru held forth for about three quarters of an hour and gave a full account of events in Kashmir as he saw them. **He said categorically** that, if the Dominion of India had not gone to the assistance of Kashmir when called opon, not only by the Ruler but also by Sheikh Abdullah, the leader of the biggest popular party, he had no doubt whatever that **the present Government of India would have been replaced by an irresponsible and extremist Government which, in his opinion, would probably have declared war upon Pakistan.**'

The Socialist Rupublican, Vol.I, Saturday, 8th Nov. 1947, No. 3 reveals: Is it Pakistan invading Kashmir? The impression created in the minds of the lay public in the Dominion of India, at least in the early stages, is that Pakistan is the aggressor and has launched upon a career of loot and conquest. And then without an explanatory preface a news item from New Delhi contradicts this impression and categorically says that "**Pakistan has no connection with the raiders.**" This contradiction again has been largely amended and modified in the subsequent press bulletin from New Delhi and in the statements of Pandit Jawaharlal Nehru himself. "We have a right to ask the Pakistan Government" says the Prime Minister of Dominion of India, "how and why these people" (the invaders) could come across the Frontier Province or West Punjab and how they have been armed so effectively. Is this not a violation of International Law and an unfriendly act towards a neighbour country? Is the Pakistan Government too weak to prevent armies marching across its territory to invade another country or is it willing that this should happen? There is no third alternative. **We do not know if there is any third alternative, because we do not know as yet as to who the invaders are.** They are often described as mere "raiders" without any other qualification or description. Sometimes they are named as "tribesmen": often enough the raiders become, unobtrusively, "tribesmen and other invaders." But then, the invaders were no mere irregular bands, but well armed men led by commanders who were using ground tactics learnt during last World War they were provided with motor transport. And, again, unobtrusively, the conclussion is reached that "the invasion was fully aided," if not actually sponsored and organised by Pakistan.

It is said that "Sardar Mahammed Ibrahim, Head of Provisional Government of Azad Kashmir" has asked for UNO's arbitration in Kashmir, and, has solicited President Truman's and Marshall Stalin's help. Has Pandit Jawaharlal Nehru explored truth sufficiently thoroughly and exhausted the range of possibilities before declaring 'There is no Third Alternative?' The names of certain leaders of I.N.A. notably of Major General Kiani, and of Col. Habibur Rahaman Khan have been mentioned in the press as leading the invasion. Mahatma Gandhi in his post-prayer speeches naturally has blessed Pandit Nehru and also the owners of Dakota Planes for timely military assistance to the Kashmir State and has naturally again, reproached the I.N.A. leaders for participation in the campaign of loot and arson. Shall we be forced by the course of events to think of Major General Kiani or of Col. Habibur Rahaman as belying the I.N.A. saga? Shall we be compelled to think as mere professional soldiers unaffected by idealism or as conscious or unconscious agents and instruments of cruelty and communalism?We have to ask- Is there a third alternative?'

Then there comes a story of a mysterious Sanyasi behind Kashmir's accession to India. Ramchandra Kak was the Prime Minister from June 30, 1945, to August 11, 1947, when he was sacked, arrested, and tried on false charges. Initially, Maharaja Hari Singh was liberal and free from religious prejudices, but he came under the sway of Swami Sant Dev. When Nehru came to Kashmir for the second time in 1946, he visited him, an old friend (*Selected Works of Jawaharlal Nehru*, First Series, Volume 15; p 418).

Kak writes: The Maharaja believed that after the departure of the British from India, he would through the potency of the Swami's supernatural powers, be able to extend his territory and rule over a much larger dominion than that already comprised in the Jammu and Kashmir State. A good deal of propaganda was being carried on in the State and in the Punjab, about the formation of what some people then called Dogristan, in which it was hoped to include, besides the Jammu and Kashmir State, the districts of Kangra and the States and areas now mostly included in Himachal Pradesh. Kak was not forgiven for administering a cold douche to the idea. The Swami was pro-Congress and launched a parallel diplomatic channel. Kak recorded these developments in detail in a note he submitted to Hari Singh on July 30, 1947, which he has reproduced in full in his Note of 1956. The Swami parted company with Hari Singh when they left Srinagar for Jammu.

Kak's version on this episode also is supported, this time, by Dr. Karan Singh (Son of Maharaja Hari Singh) in his autobiography, *Heir Apparent* (Oxford University Press; 37): A strange development took place in our household. A certain Swami Sant Dev, who had lived in the State decades earlier in the time of the late ruler, Maharaja Pratap Singh, and was reported to have been banished by my father when he ascended the throne, staged a mysterious comeback. My father was far from being a religious man, but to everyone's amazement, he suddenly became a devout disciple of Swamiji, sitting for long periods on the ground before him and never smoking in his presence.

Swamiji was presented by him with lovely silk robes, a silver hookah, and many other amenities, including a car. He was a remarkable man in many ways, erudite in several fields of knowledge and pink-complexioned even in his advanced age. He would never actually reveal how old he was, but it was rumoured that he was well over eighty (some claimed a hundred).

It was in the political sphere that Swamiji's influence proved to be disastrous. As with many of the larger Indian States, the prospect of becoming an independent ruler after the British withdrawal was an alluring one for my father. It was on this feudal ambition that Swamiji astutely played, planting in my father's mind visions of an extended kingdom sweeping down to Lahore itself, where our ancestor Maharaja Gulab Singh and his brothers Raja Dhian Singh and Raja Suchet Singh had played such a crucial role a century earlier. There is also some reason to believe that Swamiji was in touch with some of the Congress leaders, and that Acharya Kriplani's visit to the State early in 1947 was a direct result of his intervention. Another visitor to Srinagar was A.S.B. Shah, Pakistan's States Minister, who warned the Frontier's Chief Minister, Abdul Qayum, on October 18 that aggression on Kashmir would provoke Hari Singh's accession to India, which it did (R.J. Noore; *Making the New Commonwealth*; Oxford University Press; p 50). Jinnah was fully aware of it. He had heard of it 15 days earlier but preferred not to be told much. Don't tell me anything about it (ibid. p 51). Tacit consent was not concealed.

CHAPTER FOURTEEN

Kashmir Accedes To India

Although Kashmir, bounded by Pakistan, the Soviet Union, Tibet, and China, was India's second largest princely state, the Indian government was said to be not anxious for it to join the Indian Union. It was connected to the Indian Union by only a small neck of land. In 1947, after India gained independence from British rule, Jammu and Kashmir had the option of joining one of the new dominions, India and Pakistan, or remaining independent. The ruler of Kashmir Maharaja Hari Singh had not decided which way he wanted to go. He opted to remain independent for the immediate future since the dominions were beset with partition violence. Historical accounts suggest that he might have been contemplating independence as well. Culturally, emotionally, and historically, India, of course, had an impeccably strong case for Kashmir to be its part.

In October 1947, Hari Singh faced an armed uprising in Poonch, followed by a Pashtun tribal invasion. Soon tens of thousands of troops and tribesmen forcibly occupied the region of Gilgit-Baltistan and Mirpur and Muzaffarabad.

On the night of 24 October 1947, the Government of Kashmir appealed to the Government of India for military help and recognition of its accession to the Indian Union. India's British Governor-General, Lord Mountbatten advised the Maharaja to accede to India before India could send its troops. The Maharaja signed the Instrument of Accession on 26 October 1947, joining the princely state to the Dominion of India. The decision to send troops was taken by the Government of India on the afternoon of October 26.

The first contingent left at the day-break of Oct. 27. Since then troops and equipment were being flown over daily. The Indian Government commandeered every available Dacota in the country and steady streams of troops and supplies were being flown to Srinagar. Indian troops inflicted heavy casualties on the raiders. The raiders resorted to guerilla tactics and dispersed into the mountains. Kashmir people were responding to volunteer and 15,000 were already being given hurried military training.

It was said, "Economically Kashmir depends for its market much more on Indie than on Pakistan. Politically it was felt that India was a much more progressive State than Pakistan and Kashmir would have far greater scope for free development, according to its own genius, if she was allied to India."

Prime Minister of Kashmir Mr Meharchand Mahajan, former Judge of the Lahore High Court, was having consultations with Jawaharlal Nehru, Sardar Patel, and Sardar Baldev Singh, Defence Minister on the dramatic developments following the surprise raid by Afridi tribesmen across the Hazara border insisted by Pakistan army troops on leave in Kashmir and others -10,000 strong, armed with the latest automatic weapons.

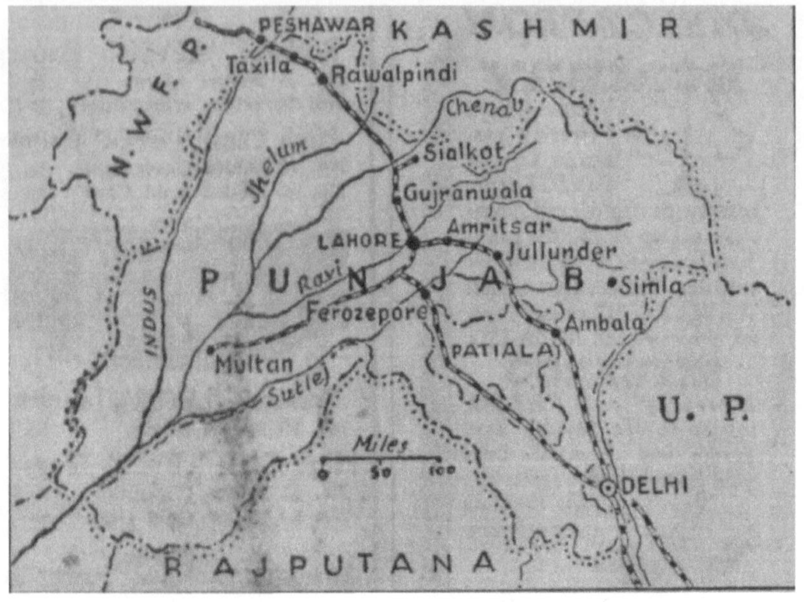

[Kashmir: Strategic importance for the security of India]

The Premier interviewed said: "Yes they have penetrated Kashmir Valley but we are holding on." He added: "Wait a day or two," suggesting that other developments might take place. Mahajan was returning to Jammu, the winter capital of Kashmir 25 miles from the Pakistan border from boundaries presumably to meet the Maharaja New Delhi.

KASHMIR ACCEDES TO INDIA: MILITARY AID SENT

[Amrita Bazar Patrika: 28 October 1947]

Observers felt "Pakistan having thrown Kashmir into the lap of the Indian Union, the Ruler may not delay announcing accession to India thus making obligatory to the Indian Government to defend the integrity of the ceding state as Jammu, Kashmir Territory after accession becomes an Indian Union territory."

The All-day consultations on the Kashmir situation on the highest level were kept "top secret," but it was common talk in the town that the Indian Union would rush help to the State Authorities including the despatch of troops if necessary. Fairly reliable sources indicated the advance of a band of raiders about 35 miles from Srinagar, the summer capital near Baramoola.

As many as 100 villages were raided, burned, and looted and women were abducted in large numbers on Oct. 12 and 24, when the main attack was launched from the North-West Frontier Province, along Abbottabad Road. Some localities like Kotli-Bhimbhar, Manawar, and Chanor were raided three times, and heavy casualties were reported. These attacks were motivated to disperse Kashmir state forces and enable the big offensive on Oct. 24.The result was the raiders moved fast in trucks, occupying Kohala, Domel, Uri, and eventually Baramulla and Patten, without serious opposition.

First armed resistance came at Uri, before Baramulla, which delayed the scheduled occupation of Srinagar, fixed for Oct. 26, the day of the Muslim festival of Id." There was to be a victory parade in the presence of the Governor General of Pakistan Mr. Jinnah on Monday, Oct 27 according to information received in New Delhi.

The first batch of Indian troops landed and launched a surprise attack on Oct 27 on the positions at Baramulla, inflicting heavy casualties.At that spot, the Indian Commander Lt. Col. Rai was killed. while his troops were withdrawing against an outflanking movement. They saved Srinagar however, which had not yet been attacked.

"India and Pakistan came within an ace of war on October 27 on the Kashmir situation," writes the special correspondent of the "Indian News Chronicle".

'It appeared that when Mr. Jinnah, Governor-General of Pakistan, heard of Kashmir's accession to the Indian Union and landing of Indian troops in Srinagar, adds the correspondent, he rang up the Acting Commander-in-Chief of the Pakistan Army and issued orders to him to move Pakistan troops to Kashmir. The Acting Commander-in-Chief in reply drew Mr. Jinnah's attention to the fact that that would mean war on the Indian Dominion.'

The raiders and Indian troops were entrenched around Pattan-Baramula-Kasemr Road, but daily and repeated strafing by Spitfires of the Indian Air Force was causing confusion to the raiders, led by experienced commanders, who belonged to the Indian National Army of Netaji Subhas Chandra Bose.

The Indian Government had promised to keep out the invading tribesmen like Afridis, Mashuds, and Waziris.

Indian troops in Kashmir to defend the invaders[Amrita Bazar Patrika: 08 November 1947]

Indian troops arrived at the Jammu border by an overland route, presumably carrying heavy arms including artillery.Hills surrounding Srinagar Valley often become snowcapped towards the end of November Before this time, it was expected the situation would be stabilised and the ralliers repelled across the Pakistan borders.

One estimate mentions the raiders' casualties as more than 1,000 against a few Indan troops. Among the Pathan raiders taken prisoner, some were reported wearing Pakistan Army uniforms. Official quarters, however, were reticent.

On 28 October 1947, it was revealed in New Delhi that Kashmir State had acceded to the Union of India. Kashmir's accession was revealed with the publication of correspondence between Sri Hari Singh, Maharajah of the State, and Lord Mountbatten, Governor General of India, shortly after Kashmir State troops were reported to have repulsed armed tribesmen advancing into the country. Earlier the Kashmir Government had asked the Government of India for help in resisting the "invasion" of armed tribesmen,

The news of Kashmir's accession to India followed reports that reinforcements of Sikh Troops from New Delhi had landed at Srinagar, the capital of Kashmir and that both the capital and its airfield were safe. Several civil aircraft, it was understood had been taken over by the Government of India to transport men and supplies to Srinagar. Order for reinforcements was to be sent followed by a meeting of the Defence Council in New Delhi on 29 October.

Things were not yet normal and the situation could not be fully controlled so soon. But the fact was that the invaders had been thrown back. A moral dam had been built against the Pakistani typhoon. Entire India's moral strength stood behind Kashmir. Accession to the Indian Union had saved the fair land from rape and rapine.

On 2nd November, Mahatma Gandhi blamed Pakistan and said, he could not understand why the freebooters in Kashmir were being led by two ex-officers of the Azad Hind.

The High Commission for India, Mr. V. K. Krishna Menon, told his first conference with representatives of the world press in London that the inescapable conclusions on the situation in Kashmir were that the passage of the invaders into Kashmir had the sanction or connivance of the Pakistan Government, or the latter had not the desire or the power to stop them.

The invaders were heavily armed with small arms, but the fact that they also had trench mortars, machine- guns, and even flame throwers, showed without the slightest doubt that there was a proper organization behind them. It was wrong to call it a raid, it was all invasion.

These were also the most charitable conclusions, added Mr. Menon. The invaders could not have got into Kashmir except through Pakistan, and there were large formations of Pakistan troops in the various through which the raiders had gone.

Mr. Menon said the Government of India had persuaded the Maharaja, Sir Hari Singh, to abide by the will of the people of the state both in regard to the internal organization of the country and its relations with the neighbouring States.

Questioned as to where the flame-throwers used by the invaders came from, Mr Menon replied: "They are not made in India. They may have come from army dumps. They came through Pakistan territory, but we are not prepared to say from which locality." Asked if he could indicate whether any other Power outside India and Pakistan was interested in getting arms into Kashmir, Mr Menon said, "No." The question, he added, was not where the arms came from, out who brought them here.

Areas infiltrated by the Raiders and pushed back by the Indian Army[Amrita Bazar Patrika: 15 November 1947]

The award-winning documentary maker Iqbal Chand Malhotra writes in his book "Dark Secrets -Politics, Intrigue and Proxy Wars in Kashmir" (Bloomsbury): "It is my calculated assessment that Prime Minister Nehru was wedged between a rock and a hard place by Lord Mountbatten or some other agents of the British Crown: either halt the Indian Army's advance into the Gilgit Agency (where the British monitoring stations were located) and accept the de facto partition of the state of Jammu and Kashmir or retake the Gilgit Agency but enter into a political and military alliance with the British Crown that would permit the British government to continue to operate its own military facilities in India for as long as they chose to do so." Nehru prevailed upon Patel, his Home Minister, to accede to the first choice.

"The entire war was a mockery that enabled Pakistan to hold on to the Muzaffarabad-Poonch belt and the Gilgit Agency, purely as a result of British perfidy. In the last week of October 1948, Nehru had spent four days relaxing in the Mountbatten country seat of Broadlands in Hampshire. "Since Mountbatten was busy with other matters in London, he left Nehru alone with Edwina Mountbatten. Edwina was to work on Nehru to accept a ceasefire in Kashmir," and on November 22, the British High Commissioner, Lieutenant General Sir Archibald Nye, met Nehru "and was able to convince him of the virtues of a ceasefire," Malhotra writes. Since then Jammu and Kashmir has been an integral part of India.

"It appears that wittingly or unwittingly, Nehru was part of the plot to restrain the Indian Army from recovering the entire Muzaffarabad-Poonch belt and the Gilgit Agency. Legendary journalist Kuldip Nayar asked (Major General) Kulwant Singh (Commander of the force tasked with beating back the infiltrators) why he restrained the Indian Army from recovering these territories. Singh replied that he had been told by Nehru to halt the Indian Army's advance at a place where the Kashmiri language was no longer spoken.

Gen. Cariappa led the Indian Army in Kashmir during the first war with Pakistan in 1947. Air Marshal K. C. Cariappa recalls his father, the first Commander-in-Chief of the Indian Army, Field Marshal K. M. Cariappa often being asked why the army did not evict the frontier tribesmen who, supported by the Pakistan Army, attacked India. The General used to reiterate that the government dictated policy. The Army was quite confident of clearing Kashmir. But the orders were to "cease fire midnight 31st December/1st January 1948-49."

Later, Gen. Cariappa asked Nehru the reasons for the ceasefire.

"You see, U.N. Security Council felt that if we go any further it may precipitate a war. So, in response to their request we agreed to a ceasefire," Nehru said. But he sportily added, "Quite frankly, looking back, we should have given you ten-fifteen days more. Things would have been different then."

The first group of United Nations military observers arrived in the mission area on 24 January 1949 to supervise the ceasefire between India and Pakistan in the State of Jammu and Kashmir. These observers, under the command of the Military Adviser appointed by the UN Secretary-General, formed the nucleus of the United Nations Military Observer Group in India and Pakistan (UNMOGIP).

Attempts by Pakistan to change the status quo have been repeatedly thwarted by India. Pakistan, however, continues to illegally occupy one part of Kashmir, PoK.

'Linked With Chandra Bose'

In 1956, the government constituted a committee to look into the circumstances around Subhas Chandra Bose's death with Shah Nawaz Khan as the head. One L.N. Roy Chowdhury from Berhampore, District Murshidabad, West Bengal, wrote letters to Shah Nawaz.

In one letter, he writes: "... think those people are silent awaiting your report or they are going to expose the true fact that Netaji is still living and at a place unknown to us. I met certain Burmese and Bengalis at Kamaut (Kamayut, Myanmar) and Achin (Auchin, Myanmar) villages who helped Netaji and INA in all respects and they gave me certain information which proved that Netaji did not meet with any accident; official correspondence also proved that he was still living then and that accident & death news was quite false. I believe that our Netaji is still living.

... In the last part of 1946 and early in 1947 when I came back to India, sometime before Independence a report came to my knowledge through official sources (Intelligence Report of the Army), It later came out in certain Newspaper as well, that**"An Indian Raja in disguise of a Fakir, with some followers, is often seen roaming about along the Himalayan Range through No man's land; sometimes seen moving from Tibbet to Bhutan and Bhutan to Tibet. He is with long hair and a beard and his followers call him Raja. From his suspicious move and** appearance, he seems to be Subhas Bose."

You may also know that both the British Govt and the Indian Govt after Independence/partition tried to follow him to find out his identity. But all met with failure. In the meantime, Tibbet has become a Free Republic State and friendly with the new China. From the above report, the general public has presumed that this has been done through Netaji."

"An Indian Raja in disguise of a Fakir..." These words of Roy Chowdhury remind us that in mid-June, 1946, the Scotland Yard and Indian Police authorities were maintaining a vigilant watch along the entire India-Burma border to capture Subhas Chandra Bose who had been reported 'dead' and the travellers crossing the border were being subjected to a careful check and asked if they have seen a bearded Indian Rajah dressed as a fakir.

Declassified File No. C/125/11/69/JP, Ministry of External Affairs, East India Division Section, reveals that one Iqbal Bahadur Saxena from Gorakh Park, Shahdra, Delhi 6, published a series of sensational news in his weekly newspaper, *Viswa Neta (Saptahik)*.

In Issue No. 74, Saxena reported that he had filed a case under Section 420, 120 of the Indian Penal Code concerning Netaji Subhas Chandra Bose in New Delhi Court against Uttam Chand Malhotra and others, who were to appear in the Court. He published a statement of one Baba Hari Charan Giri, a religious preacher, and resident of Goshala, Delhi [Translated from Hindi]:

Netaji seen in Nepal in 1949

Met Netaji again in 1968

"I know the complainant and the accused. I was the guru or priest of Netaji Subhash Chandra Bose's house. ...After he disappeared from India in 1941, **Netaji met me again in Nepal in 1949, when King Tribhuvan Bir Bikram Shah Dev Adhiraj took refuge from the**

Indian Government. Had asked for it and he had come to Delhi, while there Nepal launched an armed fight against Rana Shahi due to his spreading influence.

Netaji met me in Trihi Brahmdev mandi which is a business market of Nepal. I was sitting in meditation and thinking about how to overthrow the kingdom of this Rana Shahi. **On this occasion, Netaji stayed with me for a full 8 hours.In October 1949, he suggested a confidential idea to me and told me quietly how to wage war against Rana Shahi.** I meditated as per the suggestion given by Netaji Subhas Chandra Bose and got help in the task of overthrowing the kingdom of Rana Shahi in Nepal. At that time, I was the Nepalese war representative and also the surveyor of this war. I kept this war going for two whole years and only in 1951, what happened was that we got help in ending the rule of Rana Shahi in Nepal. We established Congress rule in Nepal and called back the King of Nepal.

After explaining his views in detail in October 1949, he promised to see us on the day when we would be successful in our work. So in June 1951, after meeting at Chaur he congratulated us on our great success. He did not say anything to me. **After that Netaji wanted to go to Tibet.** I told my messenger to accompany Netaji to the border. I brought Netaji safely to the border of Chaur Tibet. **Again I met Netaji in September 1968. I met Subhash Chandra Bose on the border of Tibet. Netaji stayed with us for 3 days in Tehsil Saharanpur, District Rampur (Uttar Pradesh). Netaji can not appear as Subhas Chandra Bose in public with a clean moustache only for one reason, he has been declared dead by the Indian Parliament andsecondly, he is a war criminal.** This Shah Nawaj Commission report is useless and worthless. I know where Netaji is at present but don't want him to violate the security rules."

It may sound incredible, but it does point to Bose's link to important events in world politics that followed 1945. This could mean that he was alive and not confined to Russia before or after the 1950s. Let's briefly discuss his possible movements in Nepal,

Tibet, and China during this period.

According to the priest, Baba Hari Charan Giri, he met Netaji in Nepal in October 1949. Tamil Nadu's former MLA A.R. Perumal, in his book '*Mudisooda Mannar Pasumpon Muthuramalinga Thevar*', has revealed that during a public meeting held at the Tamukkam ground in Madurai on 23 January 1949 in connection with birthday anniversary celebrations of Bose, freedom fighter and former Tamilnadu president of All India Forward Bloc, Pasumpon Muthuramalinga Thevar -the staunch Bose follower announced: *"Netaji is well and safe. It is false that our leader Netaji died in the air crash. Our leader will appear before the people at the right time. Besides, I am in direct contact with Netaji."*

On November 12, 1950, *The Evening Star,* one of the US's premier afternoon newspapers reported a piece of sensational news **'Linked With Chandra Bose.'**

In reality, a revolt flared on November 11, 1950, in Nepal even as deposed King Tribhuvan Bir Bikram and his two queens arrived by plane in New Delhi to begin a life in exile.

The Nepalese Congress Party was one of the agencies struggling for increased democratic rule in Nepal a move also desired by King Tribhuvan Bir Bikram. The monarch fled to the Indian Embassy in Kathmandu with his two wives and several other members of his family.

The Nepalese embassy in New Delhi announced that raiders numbering 200, who travelled in trucks, clashed with Nepalese militia at Birgunj to capture the military barracks. As a buffer between the part of India and Communist-invaded Tibet, Nepal was a geo-strategically important state. Birgunj, a city of Nepal is attached in the North to Raxaul on the border of the Indian state of Bihar. It lies 60 airline miles south of Kathmandu.

The raid was made by armed supporters of the Nepalese Congress Party and they captured the district governor and his family. The governor was a supporter of Prime Minister Surendra Bikram Shah, the "strong man" of the autocratic Nepalese government who broke the king.

The Nepalese embassy said some of the raiders were former soldiers who fought Allied troops in Malaya and Burma under Netaji Subhas Chandra Bose in World War II.

The Nepali Congress was planning to start a movement against the government of Nepal, a rumour had been heard for some time, but the public could not imagine that the movement would turn into such an armed mass uprising. **Observers felt that it would not have been possible for the Nepali Congress workers to launch armed attacks without well-planned organization and continuous military training at secret centers. It was popularly believed that a prominent part of the Nepali Congress forces formerly belonged to the Indian National Army formed by Subhash Chandra Bose. The people of Raxaul and Birgunj were surprised and terrified by the news of the armed mass coup in Nepal.**

The Nepali Congress was formed in 1947, and since its formation, the organization continuously fought for the establishment of a democratic government in the state of Nepal. A few of those who agitated within the state were sentenced to life imprisonment and those outside were ordered to be shot on sight.

After King Tribhuvan fled to the Indian embassy, the Nepali Congress Party launched a military wing called the Nepali Congress's Liberation Army and started an armed uprising against the Rana rule.

Calling upon the Nepali people who were suffering from the Rana's rule for almost one hundred and fifty years, the Chairman of a huge mass rally, Shri D.P. Pradhan said in Calcutta-**Just as Netaji, the leader of the Indian National Army, had once called for the freedom-loving Indian soldiers, today the same call has come from the border of Birgunj. In those distant mountains, our homeland -"Kathmandu Chalo."**

The people of Nepal under the Rana were suffering the atrocities. The soldiers of the freedom movement were sacrificed on the gallows, since 1941. The condition of the ordinary Nepalese people who were sometimes seen roaming around in Calcutta, was deplorable. About thirty four lakh Nepalis were living the life of animals. They had to do low-paid jobs in various parts of India. Every year, at least ten thousand Nepalis had to leave their homeland and stand at the door of India like beggars.

He said, some parts of Nepal were free and the "Liberation Army" would reach Kathmandu in a few days.He appealed to every Nepali to take an active part in the movement to establish and build democracy in Nepal and now Asia was gaining new shape and power. They wanted a real alliance with India so that Nepal could move forward together with the end of Rana shahi.

The Nepalese government launched an attack to wrest Birgunj the "Gateway of Nepal" from the rebels by thousands of troops, but the Nepal Congress troops repulsed their attack and advanced three miles north of Parwanipur before sunset. A fierce battle was fought between both sides. **Puran Singh, an ex-Major of the Indian National Army took charge of the Parwanipur rebels.**

The government forces came from nearby districts and repulsed an attack by the rebels on the town of Jaleshwar, a hundred miles east of Birgunj. The attack of insurgents on Sarlahi between Birgunj and Jaleshwar and three other police stations in the region.

Nepali Congress soon took control over three hundred villages located in 400 square miles of Juria in western Nepal. Senior police officers from Uttar Pradesh and Bihar were visiting the border areas. A huge number of police were deployed. The rebels alleged that arms and money were seized from them.

Many veterans of World War and many experienced soldiers of the Indian National Army, determined to keep hold of Birgunj, were among the rebels fighting from the southern side of Sirsiya River. A militia consisting of a few men of the Indian National Army, a few of its Gurkhas, and mainly ordinary people attacked in the form of spearheads and virtually captured Bhairahawa, east of Kathmandu.

The "Liberation Army" consisting of ex-soldiers of the Indian National Army of Subhas Chandra Bose, was a well-planned organization after continuous military training at secret centers.

The ex-I.N.A. commander Major Puran Singh took charge of the Parwanipur rebels. A fierce battle continued but finally, the Delhi Accord officially brought about the end of the revolution in 1951.

It was a compromise between the Rana's, King Tribhuvan, and Nepali Congress, which allowed for the creation of a government of a mix between Rana's and Nepali Congress members.

Though Dr. K.I. Singh who earlier had fought for the Indian National Army, was asked to stop the fighting, but he refused to accept the Delhi Accord. Dissatisfied with the leadership of the Nepali Congress, he launched another unsuccessful attack on Bhairawa. He was soon arrested in February 1951 by Indian and Nepali troops and was imprisoned in Kathmandu.

Then on 3rd May 1951, R.S. Ruikar, in a statement endorsing the statement made by Phizu, the President of the Naga National Council and one of the chief advisers of Netaji in the I.N.A.'s historical march on Manipur, said that **"Netaji is still alive and would return to India at an early date."**

The priest, Baba Hari Charan Giri said he met Subhas Bose again in June 1951. The events exactly match his statement published in Issue No. 74 of *Viswa Neta (Saptahik)*.

In January 1952, Dr. K.I. Singh broke out of prison in Kathmandu and attempted a coup, failing which he and 37 of his followers left for Tibet.

Mawu Angami, a Naga political leader associated with Phizu for several years and detained in the Special Jail, Nowgong (Assam) was examined as a witness (witness No. 202) by the G.D. Khosla Commission of Inquiry. In the inquiry report, there is about a news item that was published by *Hindustan Standard* on September 2, 1957, and was as follows:

"That Netaji Subhas Chandra Bose is alive and he had a high level conference with Phizo, Naga rebel leader, somewhere in Indo-Tibet border in 1952, understood to have been said by Mawu, personal envoy to Phizo recently arrested in Damcherra Chama while returning to Nagaland from Pakistan."

Netaji To Return To India Soon

RUIKAR'S HOPE

Naga Leader's Statement Endorsed

NAGPUR, MAY 3.—Sri R. R. Ruikar, General Secretary, All-India Forward Bloc, in a statement today endorsing the recent statement made by Sri Phizu, the President of the Naga National Council and one of the chief advisers of Netaji in the I.N.A.'s historical march on Manipur, that "the story of air-crash and Netaji's alleged death therein is a pure myth", said :

"All the evidence that has been placed before us, both by official and non-official sources leads us to the irresistible conclusion that Netaji did not die in the air crash."

Sri Phizu's statement, Sri Ruikar added, made it perfectly clear that Netaji was still alive and would return to India at an early date.—U.P.I.

[Hindustan Standard: 05-05-1951]

However, according to the inquiry report, when Mawu Angami was questioned about this news item, he denied its correctness and said: "The mistake lies in the fact that I told him (a press correspondent) that meeting would be arranged and not that the meeting had taken place between Mr. Phizo and Shri Subhas Chandra Bose."

On 24 September 1952, a news item appeared on page 3 of the *National Standard*, Bombay, under the heading **"Netaji likely to turn up in Nepal, says friend."**

Mr. Mohammad Karim Ghani, a former Minister in the wartime "Azad Hind Government" reported his belief that Subhas Chandra Bose was still alive and predicted he would soon appear. Ghani, a former close associate and minister in Subhas Chandra Bose's Cabinet, strongly contended in 1946 that Bose was not killed in that crash as it was officially claimed.

He contended that based on his personal information and knowledge of Bose's horoscope, Bose's reappearance was very near. **He predicted that Bose "might show up in Nepal in the company of Dr. K.I. Singh," a Nepalese rebel who was then reported to be collaborating with the Chinese Communists in Tibet.**

Little is known of Dr. K.I.Singh's life in Tibet, except that he had supposedly asked China to help him overthrow his government. In 1955, after China and Nepal established diplomatic relations, Singh returned to Nepal.

The reclusive ascetic (sanyasi), who later was known as Bhagwanji arrived at Shringar Nagar in Lucknow's Alam Bagh area in 1955, barely two years after Stalin's death. According to Saraswati Devi, who looked after him from 1955 to 1985, Bhagwanji had entered India from Nepal with the help of her father Mahadeo Prasad Misra, a Sanskrit teacher in Nepal. Bhagwanji lived in a rented house in Shringar Nagar for two years in relative anonymity before moving to Neemsar, near the Indo-Nepal border in 1957.

Netaji Subhash Chandra Bose had long ago and repeatedly warned about the possible partition of India. We learned about the radio broadcast that he would return to the country in 1947. News about his presence in the North West Frontier Province was published in 1946 but we don't see that he could return in 1947. There are newspaper reports and statements about possible movements of the master strategist in Nepal-Tibet-China during 1949-1951 and in many other places later.

Assuming all these are facts, was his movement in 1947-1948 restricted to any particular area, in the USSR? Partition of India would not have been possible had he been present then.

After a fallout with Pandit Nehru, Dr. Shyama Prasad Mukherjee became opposed to the legislation and raised his voice against the provision of Article 370 in his Lok Sabha speech on 26 June 1952.

Shortly before his departure to Jammu from Delhi railway station, he issued a statement: "Mr. Nehru has repeatedly declared that the accession of the State of Jammu and Kashmir to India has been hundred percent complete. Yet it is strange to find that one cannot enter the state without a previous permit from the Government of India. ..."

He was arrested by Jammu and Kashmir Police on 11 May 1953 while crossing the border into Kashmir without the "permit". He was detained without trial by Sheikh Abdullah's government of Jammu and Kashmir and mysteriously died under detention at a prison in Srinagar, on 23 June 1953.

In March 1999, Shri Bijan Ghosh, Advocate of the Supreme Court of India, wrote a letter to the Ministry of Home Affairs, asking for a fresh Judicial Inquiry into Netaji Subhas Chandra Bose's "death" and White Paper w.r.t. Status of Netaji as an International War Criminal. In that letter, he demanded a fresh probe about the mysterious death of Shyama Prasad Mukherjee [Declassified File No. 915/11/C/9/99/Pol]:

"His death was not related to Kahmir but Netaji. Netaji wanted to enter India via Chitral, Gilgit (which files are till date Classified, some are lying at the National Archives).

Netaji wanted to discuss that matter and sought assistance of Shyama Prasad for an help from within India, which was the cause of death of Shyama Prasad."

CHAPTER SIXTEEN

If a leader should emerge once more

Adherents of Subhas Chandra Bose persistently claimed that 'he still lives', probably somewhere in the Soviet Union. It was reported from London on February 1, 1948, that Bose would emerge to "fill the vacuum left by Gandhi's passing" according to the members of the Subhas Society in London. Society members, K.P. Dalal from Bengal, P.S. Misra from Kashmir, and J. Haque from Pakistan reiterated this belief and said that the time was now opportune for Bose to reappear.

"His immense influence has spread all over India. If he remains alive and that is to be sure possible-the whole world, then, one day, will hear again his speech." [*28.10.1949 INTERPRESS. INTERNATIONAL BIOGRAPHIC PRESS SERVICE. PUBLICATION CODE 335/1949*]

On 27 August 1949, it was reported that Herr Hein Von, a German civilian, who during the Second World War, happened to have made first-hand efforts to ascertain the facts behind the reported death of Subhas Chandra Bos in the air crash in Formosa, observed that Netaji's reported death was a political mystery and from the knowledge he had gathered in the Far Eastern countries, he believed 'Netaji is alive'.

Ultimately getting a scent of his inquisitiveness about the news of Netaji's death, the Japanese Foreign Office asked him to desist from the pursuit saying that if he was a true friend of Netaji, he must not make any more attempts in this direction because 'Netaji's death is a Top Secret'.

In August 1952, the West Bengal Legislative Assembly unanimously adopted a non-official resolution expressing the view that the State Government should move the Government of India to take necessary steps for ascertaining "the real facts about the alleged death of Netaji Subhas Chandra Bose." The resolution was moved by Dr Kanai Bhattacharjee, a member of the Forward Bloc, and supported by all the parties including the official Congress Party. The mover accepted an amendment of the Government Chief Whip deleting a suggestion to "set up a non-official enquiry committee" for the purpose.

Thevar:	If Government says that he was never declared a war criminal, then I will go into the question. I am sure that he was declared a war criminal; his status might have changed but the suspicion is that it remains in the Commonwealth. Even if it is to remain in the Commonwealth the Government says anything I can take it for granted.

[From the Netaji enquiry committee Report: 1956]

Muthuramalinga Thevar, a firebrand nationalist whom Bose himself called the 'Bose of South', did not approve the constitution of the 'Netaji enquiry Committee' headed by Shah Nawaz Khan. The committee should have been headed by a person like Justice Dr. Radha Binod Pal (one of three Asian judges appointed to the International Military Tribunal for the Far East. Later, he was an Indian jurist member of the United Nations' International Law Commission from 1952 to 1966).

Thevar appeared before the Shah Nawaz Khan headed 'Netaji enquiry Committee' on 4 April 1956, but even after his repeated persuasions, the committee members failed to clarify the Government's position on whether Bose was declared a war criminal or not. Thevar kept mum on Bose's whereabouts.

The Intelligence Bureau reported that they had received information from a reliable source that some of the Top Secret papers of the Government of India made available to the Chairman of the Netaji Enquiry Committee were available in the possession of Sunil Krishna Gupta, 25/A, Kristo Das Pal Lane, Calcutta and it appeared that he obtained them through Shri Bose (Suresh Chandra Bose, the elder brother of Netaji Subash Chandra Bose) who was a member of the Enquiry Committee (Shah Nawaz Committee: 1956). It was also reported that Sunil Krishna Gupta intended to show those papers to his friend, Muthuramalinga Thevar.

In a letter dated August 23/24, 1956, it was brought into the notice of the Chief Secretary, Govt. of West Bengal to look into the matter whether it was necessary to search the premises of Sunil Krishna Gupta for recovery of the file.

Interestingly, he is the same Sunil Krishna Gupta, the ardent follower of Netaji Subhas Chandra Bose, who first met Bhagwanji at Naimisharanya in U.P. in 1963 and carried on meeting and correspondence with him till 1983.

In the Issue No. 74 of *Viswa Neta (Saptahik)*, Iqbal Bahadur reports a statement of one Mr. Jaikaran Sharma, from Hanuman Galo, Jind (Haryana), claiming he had witnessed a conspiracy meeting to plant Shoulmari Sadhu as Netaji [Translated from Hindi]:

"Earlier I used to live in Morigate, Delhi. Now I am in Jind (Haryana). I was working as a Malgujaari Patwari. In January 1962, I resigned from the post of Patwari. To find a better job in Delhi, I went to the then President of the Punjab Provincial Congress Committee, Mr. Bhagwat Dayal Sharma, and through him, I sent a letter to Sardar Pratap Singh Kairon, who was the Chief Minister of Punjab at that time, and a letter of introduction in the name of the then Prime Minister Jawaharlal Nehru. I took this letter which was given by Sardar Pratap Singh Kairon to Shri Jawaharlal Nehru sometime in March 1962.

When I reached Teen Murti Delhi, I was presented before Jawaharlal Nehru, about ten to twelve people were present. At that time, Shri Kamaraj, Morarji Desai, Y.B. Chauhan, Sardar Swarn Singh, P.C. Sen, and Smt Indira Gandhi were present. Apart from them, Shri Uttam Chand and Hira Lal Dixit were also present. After receiving my letter, Nehru ji asked me to sit in a corner and also said that he would talk once the meeting was over. In my presence, Nehru ji told all those present there that **Netaji Subhas Bose was released from jail in Russia. He is now roaming in or around India.** He was speaking in Hindi, and he (Nehru ji) said, "If Netaji comes forward openly then they will be in trouble and the Congress Government will be finished. Morarji Desai advised that such an arrangement should made so that the Congress Government remains safe. On this, Swarn Singh advised that there is an Ashram in Bengal and its Sadhu can be made a replacement for Netaji Subhash Bose. Uttam Chand Malhotra should be allowed to go to the Ashram and after his return, it should be said in public that the Sadhu of Shoulmari Ashram is none other than Subhas Chandra Bose."

In 1962, as a result of a certain article published by Shri Uttam Chand Malhotra, a controversy arose that the Sadhu of Shaulmari Ashram was Netaji. Soon after this, Shri Surendra Mohan Ghosh, MP. went to Shaulmari Ashram and stayed there for two days. During his stay, he spent 5 hours with the Sadhu. It was his definite view that the Sadhu was not Netaji. Shri R.R. Das, Secretary of the Ashram publicly declared in October 1962 that the founder of the Shaulmari Ashram who is generally known as Swami Saradanandaji was not Subhas Chandra Bose nor had he ever had any connection whatsoever with the family in which Netaji was born. A Bengali leaflet published by the Shaulmari Ashram reiterated that the Swami was born of a Brahmin family in East Bengal and was not Netaji.

Prof. Samar Guha sent a booklet *Country must know what happened to Netaji* along with a letter dated November 21, 1992, to Shri K.R. Narayanan -the then Vice President of India and Chairman, Rajya Sabha, in which he alleged, "Shah Nawaz Committee, however, helped to have access to some very vital documents that were kept secret for 10 years after 1947.

3.   In 1962, as a result of certain articles published by Shri Uttam Chand Malhotra, a controversy arose that the Sanyasi of Shaulmari Ashram was in fact Netaji. Soon after this, Shri Surendra Mohan Ghosh, M.P. went to Shaulmari Ashram and stayed there for two days. During his stay, he spent 5 hours with the Sadhu. It was his definite view that the Sadhu is not Netaji. Shri R.R. Das, Secretary of the Ashram publicly declared in October, 1962 that the founder of the Shaulmari Ashram who is generally known as Swami Saradanandaji was not Subhash Chandra Bose nor had he ever had any connection whatsoever with the family in which Netaji was born. A Bengali leaflet published by the Shaulmari Ashram reiterated that the Swami was born of a Brahmin family in East Bengal and was not Netaji.

These documents showed that according to the intelligence report, in all probability, Netaji took shelter in Soviet Russia under the cover of a cooked-up story of his death. These documents also indicated that Gandhiji and Panditji received a letter from Netaji asking Nehru to make arrangements for his repatriation to India. Particular imports of these documents will be discussed later. But it should be mentioned here that Pandit Nehru suppressed all the vital intelligence reports from the public till 1956." [Declassified PMO Political File No. 870/11/P/16/92-POL]

CIA tracks Subhas Bose till 1964

Declassified documents show that even in 1964, at the level of the US Secretary of State, the Central Intelligence Agency (CIA) had reservations about Subhas Bose's death and was mulling over the possibility that Bose might return to his homeland.

The CIA had not been talking of some sort of a resurrection. It simply never believed that Bose died in Taiwan. In its incarnation as the Office of Strategic Service (OSS), it had been keeping a close watch on Bose's daring moves after his great escape from Calcutta in 1941.

A memorandum to the State Department on July 1946, almost a year after Bose's 'death', states that "a search of our files indicates that there is no information available regarding subject's (Bose's) death that would shed any light on the reliability of the reports mentioned in the reference inquiry to the State Department".

Earlier, in May 1946, an airgram to the Secretary of State dwelt on the impact of Subhas Bose's return to India. The agent, whose name has been blacked out along with other vital details, writes that someone approached him "several days ago on the question of Subhas Chandra Bose. ... (censored) ... said that the hold which Bose had over the Indian imagination was tremendous and that if he should return to the country trouble would result which in his judgment would be extremely difficult to quell."

"According to ... (censored) ... it should be reasonably easy to establish beyond the shadow of a doubt whether Bose is dead or alive."

Originating in Bombay, the airgram was received in Washington DC on June 3, 1946, at 2.13 PM. It concludes by saying: "If the (State) Department could furnish any information on this subject (Bose's death), it would be most helpful to this Consulate General ... (censored) ... positive proof of some kind that Bose is dead would be most interesting."

However, it is the documents of the 1964 vintage that are most astonishing. That the CIA should even discuss Subhas's 'return' in the 20th year of his 'death' is quite astonishing. Dated February 27, 1964, and heavily censored, this particular document just about manages to import the crux of the matter.

It is a memorandum for "Chief, ... (censored) ..." and the sender is Deputy Director of Security. The subject has been blacked out but Subhas Bose's name appears in ink. The document reads as follows:

1. Reference is made to your telephonic request of 19 February 1964 that the Subject be interviewed by a representative of this office.

2. Attached is the report of the interview conducted on 27 February 1964 at Washington DC No further action will be taken in this matter unless requested by you.

The document carries the following attachments:

"At Washington DC: On February 26, 1964, at approximately 1345 hours, ...(censored)...was interviewed...(censored)...? ...(censored)... relate a story concerning the possible return of one Subas (or Subhas) Chandra Bose. This individual is a former deposed president of the Indian National Congress, 1938-39, and is believed to have died in an airplane crash after the war. However, there now exists a strong possibility that BOSE is leading the religious group undermining the current Nehru Government."

"Subject desired that his story be presented to the proper persons in the agency for evaluation and to alert those concerned of the previously mentioned possibility. Subject also advised the [sic]...(censored)... was a former member of the British Counter Intelligence Corps and could provide some factual information regarding BOSE and his operations with the Indian National Army during World War II.

"SUBJECT was dressed neatly in a designer suit and his conversation was intelligent. He did not appear to be alarmed or emotional about his story and was merely offering it as a guide to the Central Intelligence Agency for whatever action they deemed advisable".

In Issue No. 75 of *Viswa Neta (Saptahik)*, Iqbal Bahadur Saxena reports another sensational news on Netaji Subhas Chandra Bose's announcement on the radio [Translated from Hindi]:

Shri Netaji Subhas Chandra Bose's announcement on the radio

There will be a revolution and it will definitely happen

According to the information received, many government and non-government citizens of Delhi listened to Netaji Shri Subhas Chandra Bose's latest speech broadcast from Peking Radio at 6 PM on the night of 20-2-66, the outline of which was as follows: First a girl from Peking Radio said- "Now a warm-hearted leader of your country, Shri Subhas Chandra Bose is on the mic, now you listen to him. After a few moments, the voice of Netaji Subhas Chandra Bose was heard and he said-

I am Subhas Chandra Bose speaking.

Since the Second World War, as I have been assuring you every time while addressing you, I have full faith that India will definitely be free and there will be no power in the world that can stop us from doing this. The division that the imperialist forces have created to create division among us does not affect us because the people living in Pakistan are also our brothers. We should maintain good relations with them. They can come together again at any time, we have to embrace them, they are our blood, then how can we stay apart from them?

Now the time has come when every citizen, labourer, farmer, and political institution of India should look in this direction and make the same sacrifices to liberate themselves as those whose martyrdom was unmatched. Can be found in the history of the Second World War. There will be a revolution and it will definitely happen. It is necessary to have everyone's cooperation in this revolution. I have always been saying this, and will still say with full confidence that you give me blood and I will give you freedom. Freedom is standing in front of you. Which demands sacrifice from you, no country can become independent without making sacrifices, hence it is extremely important that we Indians present ourselves at the feet of our Mother India for sacrifice.

Jai Hind
Inquilab Zindabad
Azad Hind Zindabad

[Declassified File No. C/125/11/69/JP, Ministry of External Affairs, East India Division Section]

Suresh Chandra Bose was Subhas Chandra Bose's elder brother and the most relevant person in the context of the Netaji mystery considering that he was part of the Shah Nawaz Committee set up in 1956 to inquire into his brother's fate. From 1963, the year he came to know about Bhagwanji, Suresh Chandra Bose made repeated public statements that Subhas was alive. It was at the same time that Bose's nephew, Dwijendranath Bose also claimed in the Forward Bloc conference that Bose was not only alive at that time but also still working for India.

Then the Times of India, February 21, 1966 reports:

Netaji Alive, Says Relation

It would be true to say that "**Netaji Bose is alive today,**" according to Mr. Suresh Chandra Bose, a relation of the Netaji.

Mr. Suresh Bose, who is here to participate in the All India Forward Bloc Conference, said today that the Netaji would be back in India by next month.'

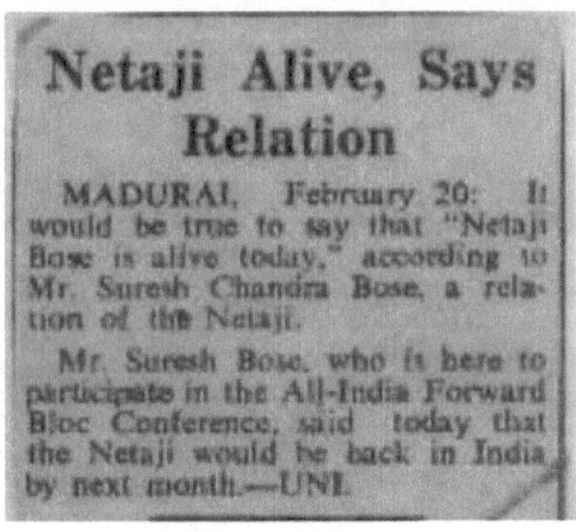

[Times of India, February 21, 1966]

On March 7, 1966, the leading newspapers like Hindustan Times, Hindustan Standard, and Amrita Bazar Patrika covered the news of claims by Shri Dwijendranath Bose.

Netaji still alive, says nephew

Mr. Dwijendranath Bose, General Secretary of the All India Forward Bloc, and a nephew of Netaji Subhas Chandra Bose reiterated here today that **Netaji was still alive and was working in a place near the borders of India.**

I can tell you that last September, Netaji had an attack of pneumonia and was examined and treated by some very eminent doctors whom I know, but I wouldn't name, Mr. Bose told reporters.

Mr. Bose also stated that a staff reporter of a Calcutta daily had gone to the place where Netaji was staying, and had returned convinced that he was alive. The reporter, of course, could not meet Netaji.

Asked why Netaji was still in hiding, Mr Bose replied that it was not correct to say that he was in hiding. He is still working for India. He will come out into the open and enter India at the appropriate time in such a way that he can establish a new order in the country,' Mr. Bose said. [Amrita Bazar Patrika: 7 March, 1966]

Taiwan Govt. probe 'Netaji mystery'

Mr. H.V. Kamath, MP, suggested here today the setting up of a tripartite committee by the Governments of India, Japan, and Taiwan to investigate the mystery of the death of Netaji Subhas Chandra Bose.

Mr. Kamath, who has returned after a visit to Taiwan, told newsmen, that the Taiwan Government, which was inquiring into the Netaji mystery, had so far failed to obtain any concrete evidence in support of the belief of a section of the people that the Netaji died in an air crash in Taiwan on Aug 18, 1945 [Hindustan Times: 24 December, 1966].

The Foreign Minister while answering a further question on this subject in the Rajya Sabha on May 17, 1966, stated that the Government had accepted the findings of the Shah Nawaz Committee and had not come across any further information that would contradict the findings of the Enquiry Committee.

Iqbal Bahadur Saxena stated that he listened to a programme over Radio Moscow on **20-1-1967** which was a speech of Netaji Subhas Chandra Bose regarding the Tashkent Agreement between Late Shri Lal Bahadur Shastri and President Ayub Khan. His letter written to the Director, of Radio Moscow, along with the reply received was published in *Viswa Neta* on 27-02-1969.

Shri Saxena further stated that the Director, Radio Moscow had accepted in the said letter the broadcast speech of Netaji. His request for supply of the recorded tape of Netaji's speech had not, however, been acceded to on the plea that this could not be done without Netaji's direct and specific permission. Shri Saxena stated that the letter made it quite clear that Netaji Subhash Chandra Bose was, in fact, alive and that he was either in Russia or in any other neighbouring country. Saxena said that the original letter was in his possession and could be produced as and when required.

(On being asked to do so, he produced the original which was returned to him after perusal). The copy was found to be correct.

On the 26th of April 1967, Saxena was further deposed, in a broadcast from Radio Moscow, it was announced that the Third World War was going to start soon and its operation would be carried by a great leader of India. This report was published in *Vishwa Neta* on **10-6-67** under:-

"Moscow -**Moscow Radio in its broadcast at 9.30 P.M. on 26-04-67 predicted that the Third World War is going to start very soon and its operation will be carried out by a very great leader of India.**"

Saxena told the Court that many questions were asked in Parliament about this broadcast from Moscow but the Government of India gave false statements regarding the broadcast. Shri Saxena cited a report published in the "Nava Bharat Times" dated 15-7-67 in this regard, as under:-

"Russia has once again informed the Government of India that the "Peace and Progress Radio Station propagating against India is not in Russia and that the Moscow Government has no knowledge about it."

Iqbal Bahadur Saxena dropped bombshells one after another in his weekly, *Viswa Neta (Saptahik)*. In Issue No. 73 of the weekly, Saxena published sensational statements given by Shyam Lal Jain, a typist from Chhopowada, Meerut (who was also steno of Mr. Asaf Ali, the then Secretary of the I.N.A. Defence Council), that Netaji Subhash Chandra Bose came to Meerut on 7 October 1967 and that he typed highly confidential letters for Nehru [Translated from Hindi]:

Leader Subhas had come to Meerut in October 1967

I typed highly confidential letters for Jawaharlal Nehru

-Shri Shyam Lal Jain Typist, Chhopowada, Meerut

On being asked by Mr. Jethanand Betav Advocate, Mr. Shyam Lal Jain (resident of Meerut) the witness said, "... I saw Netaji for the first time in 1936 and 1940 when he had become the President of the Indian National Congress and had come to Meerut on the occasion of the formation of the Forward Bloc. I am a great follower of Netaji Subhash Chandra Bose and even now I am able to recognise him.

After that, I saw him again on 7 October 1967 when Netaji Subhas Chandra Bose came to Meerut. The reason was that a Bengali gentleman named Sarkar came suddenly at 7 AM in the morning and asked about me. On my telling that I was Shyam Lal, he told me something special and said that Netaji Subhash Chandra Bose has come to Meerut and he wants to see me. At that time my son Sukumar Chand Jain was there and he too insisted on seeing Netaji. He also accompanied me. All three of us sat in the car and went to the Jadugar-ka-bagh.

There I saw Netaji sitting on the ground and smoking a cigarette. Both of them bowed in front of him and saluted him. He called me by name and said: **"Shyamlal, what are you doing these days?"** I said that I was passing my days in great trouble. **I addressed him as Netaji but he ordered me not to call him Netaji. Netaji said that he was a war criminal and that he had been declared dead by the Indian Parliament.** After that Netaji asked me to accompany him and we went to Etawah, Allahabad, and then to Mirzapur and Vindhyachal. I was with Netaji for three days in a row. And during this journey, I also had meals with Netaji and got the opportunity to talk to him several times. I know Netaji very well because I have seen him several times in 1936, 1940. It was at the end of 1945, in December, while I was working as a typist in the INA Defence Committee, I was suddenly called by Shri Jawaharlal Nehru and his staff to his house where he was behind the Daryaganj Post Office.

Shri Jawaharlal Nehru made me type a highly confidential letter in which it was stated that "On 23 August 1945, Netaji Subhas Chandra Bose came by plane from Saigon to Dairen Airport in Manchuria and landed there at 1-10 in the afternoon. After that, Netaji had breakfast of banana and tea and thereafter he sat in a motor jeep with four men, one of these men was General Shidei and I am unable to remember the name of the other Indian men now. Netaji reached the border of Russia sitting in a car." After that, Jawaharlal Nehru got a letter typed in four copies which was written to Clement Attlee, the then Prime Minister of England. It was written in it that Subhash Chandra Bose was advised by the Russians to escape and he betrayed me. Now necessary action should be taken in this matter. At that time Mr. Asaf Ali, Jawaharlal Nehru, and Indira were also present. Taking all these above points into consideration, I wrote a letter to Dr. Radhakrishnan, the then President of the Indian Colonies. ...I wrote a letter to Indira Gandhi ...I wrote another letter to Shri Y.B. Chavan, the Home Minister, Government of India, ...I wrote similar letters to Shri Morarji N. Desai, Gulzarilal Nanda, Sardar Hukum Singh, Sardar Swarn Singh

Ghaur and almost all the members of Parliament and the Congress President too, but had no effect. ..." [Declassified External Affairs/ East Asia Division Section File No. C/125/11/69/JP].

We get to know from *Charnik*'s writings that Bhagwanji stayed for some time in Nepal or adjoining areas like Pithoragarh, Almora, Nainital, Pilibhit, Khiri, Bahraich, Gonda, Basti, Gorakhpur, Deoria, Bettiah and some other places in Uttar Pradesh -was extremely dangerous for his life. His obvious safe choice of place was Vietnam. Bhagwanji laments some people from his old days were desperately in search of him, still, people believed in Falakata propaganda that the Shoulmari Sadhu was "Netaji".

In one letter, Bhagwanji -the Leader wrote to his follower Leela Roy in 1963 [14]: "*No risk can be taken to stay in those places "for some time". (You will) Lose me. Can't stay in Delhi -Meerut -Muzaffarpur -Bulandshahr -Aligarh -Etah -Mainpuri -Etawah -Lucknow -Hardai -Sitapur. Staying in Van Chinh (in Vietnam) is OBVIOUS -understand the reason. (News arrived: A few people from (my) old days + one Sikh and someone else are searching from one place to another but still believe in Falakata (?!!!) (At least that's how it's propagated to the outside world)! Understand how terrible this thing is ...*"

Bhagwanji says, "*The primary requirement is acceptance by a majority of the final and main relatives and the secondary requirement is the acceptance by a sizable number of people. ... The U.S.A., the U.K., and the European Allies know it to their Cost that, Hitler had two doubles, Stalin, also two, I personally know of Rasputin's.*". Here is a reference indicating how a planted body double gets accepted as the original one.

It's been reported: "A leading surgeon from Gorakhpur was among those who regularly visited Bhagwanji. He reportedly said, "We kept asking the Government of India to declare that Netaji was not a war criminal but our pleas fell on deaf ears. Baba did not want to emerge as a criminal. It does matter that the government did not believe in him -we did and continue to do so. We want to be known as his 'believers' because we believed in him."

In his letter dated 16-03-1968, Birendranath Chatterjee, Ex-INA approached the Members of Parliament to form an "Enquiry Commission" to [1] Find out his final programme, before he started for his mission, [2] His first starting point from Malaya & [3] His final landing to the nearest Nipponese border.

He writes:His message to the I.N.A. "We have lost this war, it was a War to help the Indian People in India from Outside, in a direct way, But I am an optimist, although the destiny was against us, but I have faith, we have won the War, because at the close of this War, no foreign rule, will remain in India, and the TRI-COLOUR will DEFINITELY, fly in INDIA & RED FORT. Secret message: Plan -To land in an airport nearest to the border of NIPPON from there through the Outer Mongolian Border -and then to U.S.S.R., but I am Afraid the snipers of the allied forces are at work, so it is left to the destiny.

Much later, a comment of theFrontier Gandhi, Badsha Khan Abdul Gaffar was published in the Oct-Nov, 1969 issue of BLITZ which is as follows: **"If a leader should emerge once more in India, who was of the people, who went to the people, who asked them what they wanted and obeyed the will of the people, the country would be saved."** [Declassified documents- SECRET: PMO Political File No. 800/6/C/3/88 -Pol Record: PMO/1/247]

Who was that leader to emerge once more in India, who was of the people? Was not the Frontier Gandhi talking about his leader Netaji Subhas Chandra Bose? Whether Bose was living incognito in different places not so distant from the border of Uttar Pradesh in the late sixties and was expected to emerge once more to save the country?

Prof Samar Guha Ex-M.P. (Lok Sabha) writes in his letter dated November 5, 1988, to Comrade Mekhail Gorbachev, the then President of the USSR, General Secretary of the CPSU Central Committee, Moscow, U.S.S.R.: "Major General Isoda and Col. Tada of the Headquarter of Field Marshall Tarauchi at Saigon, who were entrusted by Japan for ensuring safe escape of Subhas Bose from being arrested by the British Army, admitted before the

'Commission of Inquiry about Disappearance of Subhas Chandra Bose' that Japan agreed to Bose's request to airlift him to Manchuria so that he could take asylum in Russia by crossing into the Siberian territory. Accordingly, Bose was escorted to Manchuria by Gen. Shedie of the Jap Army.

Prof Samar Guha, in his letter dated 20 June 1994, writes to Prime Minister Shri P.V. Narasimha Rao: 'The British Communist leader Mr. Gallasher, who was then a member of the Parliament, said in a statement in 1949 that, "Bose has gone to Irish Free State on a secret Mission."

Deben Sen, then an M.P. made a press statement in Delhi in 1969 before his death that he and Mr. Joglaker, a founder member of the Communist Party, accidentally met Subhas Chandra Bose at Marssellies airport in France while they were going to Amsterdam to attend an International Trade Union Conference. Deben Sen, who was closely known to Subhas Chandra Bose in their ties when tried to approach Netaji at the airport, was signaled by Netaji not to approach him and keep silent as he was then found surrounded by a few Russian guards. Deben Sen on return from Amsterdam told this story to Sarat Chandra Bose and later to me privately. But he was asked by Sarat Babu not to say anything about it publicly. But in 1969, when he felt that he was about to die because of serious heart trouble, Deben Sen made a public statement in Delhi about the incident of his meeting Netaji Subhas Chandra Bose in the French airport. Interestingly, the time of this incident tallied with the time of Gallashar's statement about Netaji's visit to Ireland to meet De Valera. Unfortunately, nobody inquired from De Valera if Subhas Chandra Bose visited Ireland during the days of 1949. When De Valera later visited India, he told press people "I expected Bose to see in India."

M. Karimgani writes in his essay, *Yesterday, Today & Tomorrow* in *The Comrade* dated 17 August 1946: "Had he stayed behind, the world would have had a more sensational Trial at the Red Fort at Delhi than the Shah Nawaz Trial, and Mr. Bose might have been the Indian "Rashtrapathi" to-day in place of Mr. Nehru. But the de-

Valera policy, if at all it had benefited him, could only give him rest. However it may be, one can now hope that in the new order of things in which Dr. Ba Maw could come back to Burma as a free peacock, Mr. Bose if he wants to, could also easily come out of his lair without fear of trial or even arrest."

Eamon de-Valera was a patriot and an active anti-British Irish revolutionary who was deported in May 1918 to England and was imprisoned. After a dramatic escape in February 1919, he went in disguise to the United States, where he collected funds. He returned to Ireland before the Irish War of Independence.

<u>"NETAJI'S DEATH REMAINS A MYSTERY"</u>

The mystery has further been heightened by the recent revelation in the so-long secret document of the then Govt. of India just published in London in title "The Transfer of power" pp 42-47. Mr. R.F. Mudie the then Home Member in the Viceroy's Executive council, while replying to Mr. E.M. Jenkin's letter (Top secret No. 1157 dated August 11, 1945) regarding "Disposal of Bose" finally suggested (P 107, VOL VI) :-

"Leave him where he is and don't ask for his surrender or release", adding, "he might, of course, in certain circumstances, be welcomed by the Russian".

Again, a Central intelligence department's confidential report submitted before both the commissions held that Subhas Bose was in the Soviet Union under the assumed name of "GIZAI MILAN" a fact disclosed by the top Russian diplomats in Afghanistan and IRAN. More facts may slowly come to light to dispel doubts about the death of this redoubtable revolutionary.

— "BLITZ", JANUARY 21, 1978, PAGE-37

What could prevent a towering personality like Netaji Subhas Chandra Bose who in October 1943 declared war on Britain and the United States and gave the Indian National Army the battle cry- "On to Delhi", from coming out in the open? Any larger conspiracy under international compulsion?

The Straits Times reports on 13 January 1961: "**Britain was asked to remove the name of Subhas Chandra Bose from the list of World War II criminals before Queen Elizabeth arrives in India for a state visit on January 20**. A statement by the Subhas Chandra Bose birthday celebration central committee said that 16 years had passed since the war ended and India had achieved her freedom. It went on: "**But it is a matter of shame that Bose's name is still included in the war criminals list**." The committee has sent telegrams to the British Prime Minister, Mr. Harold Macmillan, and to the Indian Prime Minister, Mr. Nehru."

Atul Sen, who had contested the legislative seat from Dhaka in the 1930s on Netaji's insistence and won, was in 1962 traveling to various places in UP on "change" on a doctor's advice. In April, he reached Neemsar, a pilgrimage site near Lucknow. It is here that he heard from locals about a Bengali mahatma who lived in an abandoned Shiva temple. Sen's curiosity was piqued and went to meet the ascetic. He finally met him after several attempts and instantly knew it was Netaji. Over the next few days, he met Bhagwanji many times.

An ecstatic but cautious Atul Sen returned to Kolkata in 1962 and disclosed the news to Pabitra Mohan Roy, the ex-Secret Service Officer of Netaji's INA and historian R.C. Majumdar. Sen also wrote to PM Jawaharlal Nehru on August 28, 1962. "**Netaji is alive and is engaged in spiritual practice somewhere in India**... From the talks I had with him, I could understand that **he is yet regarded as enemy No. 1 of Allied powers and that there is a secret protocol that binds the Indian government to deliver him to Allied 'justice' if found alive**. If you can assure me otherwise, I may try to persuade him to return to open life," he wrote. In the reply dated August 31, 1962, Nehru denied the existence of any such protocol."

On 25 March 1963, Bhagwanji told a person called Srikant Sharma to convey to Leela Roy *My coming out is not in the country's interest. It would not do anyone any good if I emerged now.*

"London, 2nd Sept. (Reuter)—Sunday "Observer's correspondent at New Delhi declares that war councils— both British and American,— attach little credence to the Japanese news that Shri Bose has been killed in an air accident, U. S. A. has strongly resented the request made to Jahawarlal Nehru for releasing a condolatory message in honour of Shri Bose and asserted that Shri Bose should be tried as a war criminal and there were enough evidences to show that Shri Bose was found in Saigon even some days after the Japanese Radio announced his death to the world".

[PMS File No. 2(64) 56- 70 PM Vol V]

In *Charanik's* writings, Bhagwanji says [13]:"*You don't understand what vexatious dog-life the Mahakal is living. ...I am no more a man. My name has been crossed out from the human register. I am only a Token or Symbol. ...Of course, this is on cards that after these series are accomplished, the mother freeing her son from all temporal duties will keep her son hidden from the world stage.*"Nevertheless, he assures *Charanik*:"*... my Sadhana can not -shall not fail ...Matri Sadhana can never fail.*"

Shyam Lal Jain, the stenographer claimed that Netaji Subhash Chandra Bose came to Meerut on 7 October 1967 and when he met, **"Netaji said that he was a war criminal and that he had been declared dead by the Indian Parliament."**

On 22 October 1971, it was reported that the Khosla Commission of Inquiry was told that the partition between India and Pakistan would not have occurred if Netaji Subhas Chandra

Bose had been alive at the time of Independence. Hardit Singh of the Indian Independence League (IIL) added: 'Under the command of Netaji, Hindus, Muslims, Sikhs, and others ate from the same plate.'

"Netaji is still alive," said the next witness, Kashinath Yadav, ex-officer of I.N.A. He said, **"The Indian Government has still not announced that it will not try Bose as a war criminal."** He said, "When I asked Netaji how he had escaped house arrest in Calcutta, he did not answer. Instead, he told me that it was a secret which he would reveal after winning the freedom of India."

Appearing on behalf of the Bose family before the Khosla Commission, which probed Netaji's disappearance from 1970 to 1974, eminent barrister and former law minister of Bengal Niharendu Dutt Majumdar, pressed the family's view that **Netaji was yet regarded as a war criminal.**

To quote GD Khosla, "Mr. Mazumdar has, on behalf of the family of Bose, argued with considerable vehemence and persistence that the government of India has deliberately suppressed or destroyed evidence which would have proved that Bose's name was included in the list of war criminals who were to be tried by the War Crimes Tribunal."

The family told the Khosla Commission that **the charge that Bose was still a war criminal was the"most important, if not the only reason, for his remaining incognito" in the early 1970s.**

Deposing before the same commission, Pradeep Bose, another nephew of Subhas Chandra Bose insisted that N. Raghavan, Netaji's finance minister in the Azad Hind government had tried to impress upon the Nehru government that Netaji was in East Asia and was therefore posted as India's ambassador to China to find out whether Netaji was really in there. Another Netaji aide, Abid Hassan, was posted as Raghavan's first secretary. Pradeep wondered why Hassan was suddenly declared persona non grata by the Chinese.

In 1975 the British Govt. published secret documents, concerning the 'Transfer of Power' to India. In it, a specially important note, after analysing the pros and cons of various measures of how to punish Subhas Chandra Bose if he was arrested, recommended to the British Govt. in late 1945 that: "... **In many ways, the easiest course would be to leave him where he is and not to ask for his release**. He might, of course, in certain circumstances be welcomed by the Russians. This course would raise fewest immediate political difficulties." This note provides authentic information that Bose took asylum in Russia after the fall of Japan. [Declassified PMO Political File: 870/11/P/16/92/POL]

One Swami Nirvanananda of 'The True Facts and Mystery Revealing Committee', Poona, writes on 2nd August 1988, an 'ULTIMATUM' to the President of divided India with a 12 Points Charter of Demands pertaining to "NETAJI BOSE AND THE NATION":

"It was Lord Mountbatten who had diabolically demolished an INA status in Singapur in 1946 where Mr. Nehru met him.On that occasion, Mr. Mountbatten had warned Nehru not to play up Netaji or the INA for that would be tantamount to offering the premiership of India on a platter to Subhas. In the light of the above facts, one hardly finds any difficulty to understand why Netaji is remaining "incognito" and what he aspires to do. ..."

"Besides, there is another relevant factor of why Bose is silent and remaining "Incognito". War crime charges against him have still not been formally withdrawn. That status has been prolonged. For ready reference and in support of the above contention, the following one among the many other documentary evidence may be looked into:- "On November 26, 1968, the U.N. General Assembly approved the text of a convention on the Non-applicability of statutory limitation to war crimes and crimes against humanity. This is a document of great international importance. It was drafted on Poland's initiative and confirms the principle of international law, which has long since been adopted by the majority of states, under which war crimes and crimes against humanity are subject to punishment regardless of how long ago they were committed.

Leaving aside the above cited fact, on August 18, 1945, in an answer to a question at the British parliament Mr. Clement Atlee, the premier of Britain said: "There had been an agreement with the Indian leaders that whenever Subhash Babu's arrest would be secured he would be handed over to Britain." He who accepts the agreement as true points his finger to the following words gathered by experts in the field and at the same time offers to take others on his shoulder with a view to find its reason all out, "Official documents dealing with the transfer of power to India will not be officially released until 1999".

It is, therefore, now beyond the power and jurisdiction of the Government of India to trample on the rules of international law, the principles of the U.N. Charter, and agreements, which bear the signature of the Government of India. The resolution has no plenary power. ..."

"The U.S.A. has strongly resented the request made to Jawahar Lal Nehru releasing a condolatory message in honour of Mr. Bose and asserted that Bose should be treated as a WAR criminal and there was enough evidence to show that Bose was found in Saigon even somedays after the Japanese Radio announcement of his death to the world. Another prominent feature of the item is that **Netaji being treated as a war criminal and not dead, there is "no Fixed period" mentioned for Netaji to be treated as a war criminal.**

If we refer to statements in the Indian Parliament from time to time, we come across a number of incongruities and often unsatisfactory replies to clear question about Netaji. On March 25, 1965, Mr. Bhivuti Mishra, M.P. raised the issue of whether Netaji was criminal in the international sphere. This same fear was voiced by another M.P. Mr. S.M. Benerjee. To the former Sardar Swaran Singh, replied that the govt is "quite lay regarding the affair", while the late Lal Bahadur Shastri is stated to have told Mr. Banerjee "You

are talking of past history when the British Govt was in India."
Neither of these two replies can ever be considered as replies, let
alone satisfactory answers to legitimate queries.

The Govt. must unfold"official document dealing with the transfer
of power to India" which will not be officially released until
1999.We want to see VOL. VI, under the title "The transfer of
power, 1942-47" [Declassified: PMO/1/247 File No. 800/6/C/3/
88-Pol].

THE TIMES OF INDIA, LUCKNOW

Lucknow, Monday, May 12, 1997. Late City

NEWS DIGEST

Netaji not a 'war criminal'

NEW DELHI: The United Na-
tions has assured the Delhi based
Netaji Forum that it would not
use the term "war criminal"
while referring to Netaji Subhas
Chandra Bose.

Responding to the objections
by Forum chairman Air Wing
Marshall S. Goyal, the United
Nations in its missive said the secretary general was aware of the
image of Netaji in India but was
"powerless" to undo what might
have been done in the past.

[The Times of India: 12 May 1997]

In May 1997, The Times of India reported 'The United Nations has assured the Delhi-based Netaji Forum that **it would not use the term "war criminal" while referring to Netaji Subhas Chandra Bose.**

Responding to the objections by Forum Chairman Air Wing Marshall S. Goyal, the United Nations in its missive said the **secretary general was aware of the image of Netaji in India but was "powerless" to undo what might have been done in the past.'**

The news was also reported by the Dainik Jagran (Hindi Daily) on May 12, 1997 [translated from Hindi]:

Netaji is no longer a "war criminal"

The United Nations will no longer use the term 'war criminal' when referring to the name of Netaji Subhash Chandra Bose.

Air Marshal S. Goyal, President of the local Netaji Forum, said that the Forum had sent its objection in this regard to the United Nations, in response to which it has given the above assurance.

In response to this objection, the UN Secretary General has said that he is well aware of Netaji's reputation in India. But he is unable to do anything about what happened in the past.

Doesn't it mean that while referring to Subhas Chandra Bose, the United Nations used the term "War Criminal" in the past?

Now, we come back to the trails of Bhagwanji. The Central Forensic Science Laboratory (CFSL), which is under the Ministry of Home Affairs (MHA), citing Sections 8(1)(A), (E), and 11(1) of the Right to Information Act, 2005, refused to share the details of electropherogram report of the DNA sample of teeth recovered from the room at Ram Bhawan, Faizabad where Bhagwanji was staying,

India Today [dated 22 October 2022] reports: "Section 8(1) of RTI Act states that disclosure of which would prejudicially affect the sovereignty and integrity of India. The security, strategic, and economic interests of the State.

An electropherogram is a plot of results from an analysis done by electrophoresis automatic sequencing. An electropherogram provides a sequence of data that is produced by an automated DNA sequencing machine. Electropherograms may be used for deriving results from genealogical DNA testing and paternity testing.

Sayak Sen said that the CFSL rejected his RTI filed on September 24, 2022, replying that it would not share the electropherogram report based on three reasons. "...Most importantly, making it public can affect the sovereignty of India and its relationship with foreign states, Sen said."

Why would an old Bengali monk who stayed in a remote area in Uttar Pradesh matters so much to the international relations of India and cause a stir in the country if his electropherogram is made public?

Charanik writes the message of Bhagwanji [15]:*"What we are doing, will surely be fulfilled. (This only is mine, okay?) ...Fragmented Motherland Will Become Whole. ...Many maps will change. That's it! The Sadhana (pursuit) of the Ghost of the Dead will end."*

Can de-occupying Kashmir and forming Akhand Bharat (reunified Bharat) be a lifelong pursuit of any ordinary and anonymous sanyasi?

References:

1. '*Oi Mahamanab Ase*'; pp 112; Jayasree Prakashan [Translated from Bengali]
2. '*Oi Mahamanab Ase*' pp 408; Jayasree Prakashan [Translated from Bengali]
3. '*Oi Mahamanab Ase*'; pp 247-248; Jayasree Prakashan [Translated from Bengali]
4. '*Oi Mahamanab Ase -Osesh*'; pp 120; Jayasree Prakashan [Translated from Bengali]
5. '*Oi Mahamanab Ase*'; pp 415; Jayasree Prakashan [Translated from Bengali'
6. *Oi Mahamanab Ase -Osesh*'; pp 121; Jayasree Prakashan [Translated from Bengali]
7. '*Oi Mahamanab Ase*'; pp 25; Jayasree Prakashan [Translated from Bengali]
8. '*Oi Mahamanab Ase -Osesh*'; pp 127; Jayasree Prakashan [Translated from Bengali]
9. '*Oi Mahamanab Ase*'; pp 409-410; Jayasree Prakashan [Translated from Bengali]
10. '*Oi Mahamanab Ase -Osesh*'; pp 66-67; Jayasree Prakashan [Translated from Bengali]
11. '*Oi Mahamanab Ase -Osesh*'; pp 174-175; Jayasree Prakashan [Translated from Bengali]
12. '*Netaji Subhas Chandra: Kichu Bitarka -Kichu Tathya*'; pp 161-166; Jayasree Prakashan
13. '*Oi Mahamanab Ase*'; pp 82, 83; Jayasree Prakashan [Translated from Bengali]
14. '*Oi Mahamanab Ase -Osesh*'; pp 142, 143; Jayasree Prakashan [Translated from Bengali]

15. '*Oi Mahamanab Ase*'; pp 179; Jayasree Prakashan [Translated from Bengali]

16. '*Oi Mahanamanab Ase*'; pp 403; by Jayasree Prakashan

17. '*Netaji Subhas Chandra: Kichu Bitarka -Kichu Tathya*'; Vol. 3; pp 84; Jayasree Prakashan

18. https://openthemagazine.com/voices/the-tashkent-man/

19. https://timesofindia.indiatimes.com/india/gumnami-baba-mystery-deepens-

20. https://thedailyguardian.com/nehru-and-the-netaji-mystery/

21. https://www.thehindu.com/news/national/Nehru-was-persuaded-to-delay-statement

22. https://in.rediff.com/news/2001/aug/16cia.htm

23. https://www.thenews.com.pk/print/988220-major-malik-munawar-khan

24. https://www.brownpundits.com/2017/03/06/the-ina-indian-national-army

25. https://en.wikipedia.org/wiki that

26. salb.gov.sg/newspapers/digitised/page/indiandailymail19460925-1.1.2

27. https://asiatimes.com/2020/04/__trashed-50/

28. http://timesofindia.indiatimes.com/articleshow/5282221.cms

29. https://timesofindia.indiatimes.com/india/US-lost-sleep-over-Soviets-planting

30. https://salb.gov.sg/newspapers/digitised/page/indiandailymail19460925-1.1.2

31. https://www.timesnownews.com/india/article/kashmir-the-story-when-maharaja

32. https://theprint.in/theprint-profile/hari-singh-the-last-dogra-king-who-gave-jk

33. http://timesofindia.indiatimes.com/articleshow/104727961.cms?

34. https://www.jammukashmirnow.com/Encyc/2020/9/8/How-Jammu-Kashmir

35. https://www.indiatoday.in/india/story/netaji-subhash-chandra-bose-deathhttps://www.indiatoday.in/india/story/

netaji-subhash-chandra-bose-death

36. https://timesofindia.indiatimes.com/city/madurai/thevar-had-
hinted-netaji-was-alive

37. http://timesofindia.indiatimes.com/articleshow/48850772.cms

38. https://defence.in/threads/youll-be-shocked-to-know-
thoughts-of-jawaharlal-nehru-about

39. https://morungexpress.com/nehrus-acceptance-of-ceasefire-
in-1949-prevented-indian-army

40. https://peacekeeping.un.org/en/mission/unmogip

41. https://netajisubhas.org/index.php/1956/04/05/report-of-
the-shaw-nawaz-committee

42. https://timesofindia.indiatimes.com/city/kolkata/On-The-
Gumnami-Trail/articleshow/48827594.cms

43. https://en.wikipedia.org/wiki/Syama_Prasad_Mukherjee

44. https://indianexpress.com/article/opinion/columns/syama-
prasad-mookerjee-death-a-missing-inquiry-5789205/

45. Manchester Evening News, Lancashire

46. Morning Tribute

47. The Singapore Press

48. The Singapore Free Press

49. The Sphere, London

50. Liverpool Echo, Lancashire

51. Belfast News-Letter, Antrim

52. Dundee Evening Telegraph, Angus

53. Aberdeen Press and Journal, Aberdeenshire

54. Daily Herald, London

55. Kinematograph Weekly, London

56. Yorkshire Post and Leeds Intelligencer

57. Northern Daily Mail

58. The Scotsman, Midlothian

59. Western Morning News, Devon

60. Western Daily Press Bristol

61. Hartlepool Northern Daily Mail, Durham

62. Manchester Evening News, Lancashire

63. The Scotsman, Midlothian

64. Illustrated London News
65. Daily Mirror, London,
66. Coventry Evening Telegraph
67. Lincolnshire Echo
68. The Scotsman County: Midlothian
69. Civil & Military Gazette (Lahore)
70. Manchester Evening News
71. Dundee Evening Telegraph
72. The Sphere, London
73. Yorkshire Post and Leeds Intelligence
74. The Evening Star
75. Belfast Telegraph
76. Daily News (London)
77. The Dundee Evening Telegraph, Scotland
78. The Amrita Bazar Patrika
79. The Juagantar
80. Indian Reunification Association
81. Pakistan & Afghanistan Archives
82. National Archives of India